Serial
Killer
Timelines

Serial Killer Timelines

Illustrated Accounts of the World's Most Gruesome Murders

Dr. Chris McNab

Ulysses Press

Published in the U.S. by
Ulysses Press
P.O. Box 3440
Berkeley CA 94703
www.ulyssespress.com

ISBN: 978-1-56975-816-8
Library of Congress Control Number: 2010925864

Editorial and design by
Amber Books Ltd. in London, UK
www.amberbooks.co.uk

Project Editor: Michael Spilling
Design: Joe Conneally
Picture Research: Terry Forshaw
Front Cover Design: what!design @ whatweb.com

Printed in Singapore

10 9 8 7 6 5 4 3 2 1

Distributed by Publishers Group West

PICTURE CREDITS:
FRONT COVER: © istockphoto.com/Niilo Tippler
BACK COVER: John Wayne Gacy; Ted Bundy victim Georgeann Hawkins; body being removed
    from Gacy's house (all © Associated Press); Hillside Strangler Kenneth Bianchi in custody
    (© Associated Press/Saxon); Richard Ramirez (© Associated Press/Lennox McLendon)

INSIDE PAGES:
Alamy: 76 (Jochen Tack), 81 (Mirrorpix), 82/83 (Toby De Silva), 180/181 (David White), 186 (Matthew Totton)
Art-Tech/Aerospace: 122/123
Corbis: 10/11 (Sygma/Epix), 19 (Sygma/Epix), 28/29 (Reuters), 49 (Carl & Ann Purcell), 57 (Elaine Thompson/Reuters),
    98/99 (Ralf-Finn Hestoft), 101 (Sygma), 103 (Ralf-Finn Hestoft), 140 (Ron Sachs), 141 (Ron Sachs)
Corbis/Bettmann: 38/39, 42/43, 45, 63, 66, 69, 86/87, 89, 90, 92/93, 96, 115, 116, 144/145, 147, 148, 164/165,
    172/173, 175
Mary Evans Picture Library: 106, 110/111
Getty Images: 6 (Tim Boyle), 12–18 all (Terry Smith/Time & Life Pictures), 22 (Eugene Garcia/AFP), 27
    (Steve Eichner/WireImage), 46/47 (Flickr RM), 64/65 (Bill Stahl Jr./New York Daily News), 70/71
    (Seymour Wally/New York Daily News), 137 (Hulton Archive), 138/139 (Shawn Thew/AFP), 163
Kobal: 9 (Gene Page/MDP/New Market), 160 (MDP/New Market)
Mirrorpix: 130/131, 134/135
Photolibrary: 118/119
Photoshot: 20/21, 23, 41, 58/59, 72/73, 104/105, 108, 111, 124/125, 136, 167, 168, 171
Press Association Images: 8, 25 (Charles Bennett), 30 (Eamonn Clarke), 31, 34, 36/37 (Phil Noble), 51, 52/53
    (Cheryl Hatch), 61, 75 (Herbert Knosowski), 78/79, 85, 95 (Lacy Atkins), 112/113, 121, 127 (Alan Greth), 176
    (Brich), 178
Rex Features: 150/151 (KPA/Zuma), 152 (Sipa), 156/157, 158/159 (Paul Lomartire), 162 (Sipa), 182/183, 185
TopFoto: 24

CONTENTS

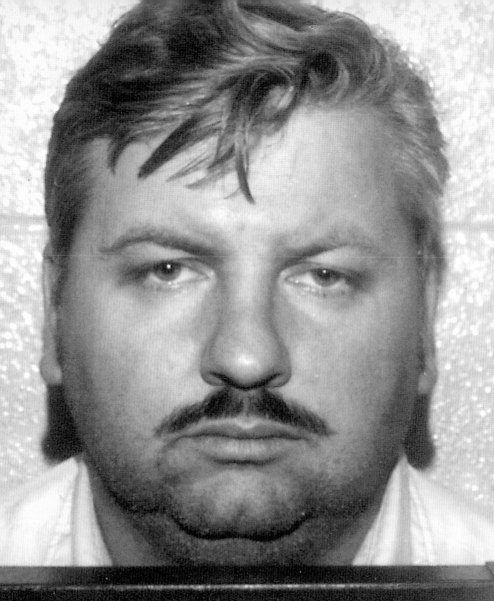

POLICE DEPT.
DES PLAINES, ILL.

78.462 12-21--78

INTRODUCTION

Scan through any weekly TV guide, and you are almost guaranteed to find a drama or documentary about serial killers somewhere among the listings. The popularity of serial killers as subject matter is not too difficult to understand. As much as their crimes are sickening and downright horrifying, the murderers are also undeniably fascinating individuals, illustrating the grotesque forms into which mind and behavior can contort.

Furthermore, serial killers usually murder over a prolonged period, generating lengthy and involved police investigations, which are forensically intriguing in their own right. Whatever our fascination with these people, however, the fact remains that we live in a world, society, and biology that still produces violent, predatory people. By definition, a serial killer is an individual who commits multiple murders over a period of time, as opposed to someone who might murder several people in one single incident. (The official FBI definition of a serial killer is a person who murders three or more people over a period of

◀ John Wayne Gacy, Jr., poses for a police mugshot shortly after his arrest in 1978. Gacy was sentenced to death in 1980 for the murder of 33 victims and executed on May 10, 1994, after 14 years in prison, launching numerous appeals against his conviction.

more than 30 days, with a "cooling off" period between each murder.) In the chapters that follow, we look at 25 landmark cases for close analysis, people whose death toll ranges from single digits through to several hundred.

Furthermore, to show that the serial killer is not a modern phenomenon, the case studies here date back to the late nineteenth century. For each murderer, we also include two timelines. One details the individual's known murders, illustrating the rhythm and pattern with which they killed. The second then gives a moment-by-moment breakdown of a particular murder, providing deeper insight into the killer's modus operandi and their psychological condition.

NATURAL BORN KILLER?

Trying to pull out the common threads that tie all serial killers together is a complicated process. Yet

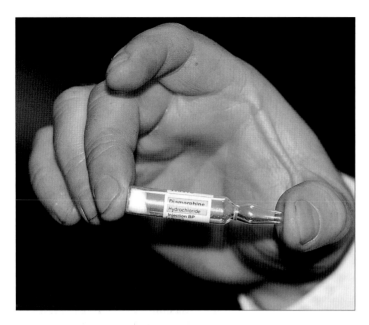

◄ A phial of diamorphine hydrochloride, the medical name for heroin. Dr. Harold Shipman was found guilty of the murder of 15 of his patients between 1995 and 1998 using injections of diamorphine.

violence. Psychologists often note that true psychosis (a disconnection from reality) is actually quite rare among serial killers; one of the reasons serial killers often stay out of the reach of the law for so long is often due to their intelligent and realistic control of their actions. Instead, a true common denominator in psychological terms appears to be a lack of empathy or guilt, expressed in the ability to inflict the most hideous pain on another individual without compunction. How this constitution is acquired, whether learned from experience or part of biological make-up, is a discussion that is far from being resolved.

TYPES OF KILLER

Although serial killers often seem to have much in common, this is not to say that they are a uniform group of people. For example, even though serial killers tend to work alone, this book contains several examples of couples who were murderers, such as Myra Hindley and Ian Brady, and Fred and Rosemary West. Furthermore, as these couples and several other entries in this book show, serial killers are not always male.

One of the most respected typologies of serial killers is that in the FBI's Crime Classification Manual, first published in 1992. It places habitual murderers into one of three categories:

Organized—These killers tend to live ordered lives, holding down jobs and social relations (often including being married and having children), and they kill in a planned, intelligent, and considered fashion. They act in ways that will inhibit subsequent investigation of their murders, such as manipulating the crime scene or controlling forensic evidence. These killers tend to possess above-average IQs.

Disorganized—Disorganized serial killers commit their murders on the basis of impulse, and hence

over recent years psychologists have identified a set of core characteristics typical of the serial killer personality and background.

Some of the key points are:

- The vast majority of serial killers—more than 90 percent—are male.
- They typically come from abusive, disturbed, or broken family backgrounds, often the victims themselves of sexual, mental, or physical abuse.
- Although they tend to be reasonably intelligent, they are generally unsuccessful in formal education.
- They perform destructive or violent acts from an early age, such as the torture of animals, arson, self-mutilation, or suicide attempts.
- Typically as a result of abuse, they grow up with distorted sexual preferences, the expression of their sexuality being linked with violent or sadistic rituals. They are usually heavy users of fetishistic or sadomasochistic pornography.

This basic checklist certainly incorporates many of the people in this book. In fact, one of the repeated tragedies of the study of serial killers is the sense that they were made rather than born, the products of early, brutal experiences.

There remains the sense, however, that this is not the whole picture, that within each serial killer is a deeper abnormality, or predisposition to

there is a more spontaneous and less controlled aspect to their violence. Often they will suddenly and compulsively perpetrate a murder, then leave the body where the killing took place without attempting to hide what they have done or significantly cover their tracks.

Mixed—A serial killer who exhibits a mixture of the Organized and Disorganized types.

Not all psychologists subscribe to this model, but similar ones are developed as its replacement. Furthermore, serial killers are often subdivided according to the motives for which they kill. Typical categories in this regard include "visionary" and "missionary"—together known as the Holmes typology, after the authors Ronald M. and Stephen T. Holmes. The visionary killer acts because he believes that he is being commanded to do so by an external force, such as God, while the missionary (or "mission-oriented") killer does so because of a desire to exterminate a certain group of people, such as homosexuals or prostitutes.

Splitting motives up further, other killers act simply because of the sexual excitement, power, or comfort they derive from causing death and mutilation. As part of the Holmes typology, an additional classification is given to how the deaths are performed, i.e., the "act-focused" murderer kills quickly and relatively efficiently, while the "process-focused" killer concentrates on the method of murder itself, typically indulging in more torture and mutilation.

Such typologies are a fascinating way of attempting to understand the nature of serial killers, and they have become important, though frequently imperfect, tools in the psychological profiling that accompanies many modern serial-killer investigations. Yet however much we attempt to understand serial killers, there seems to be something of a mystery about them, a challenge to the notion of people as civilized creatures. At the very least, they remind us that animal and violent instincts still pulse through the human character, and while the vast majority of us extinguish or suppress such instincts quite easily, there are those who give them free rein, and make our world a far more dangerous place.

▼ Actress Charlize Theron starred in the biopic *Monster*, based upon the life of Aileen Carol Wuornos, a highway prostitute who was executed for killing seven men in the state of Florida during the 1980s.

ANDREI CHIKATILO

The stories of all serial killers have the power to shock, but the tale of Andrei Chikatilo is particularly harrowing. During his lifetime he sexually assaulted and murdered at least 52 people, mostly women and children of both sexes. The reasons why his mind was twisted into such a grotesque shape can perhaps be found in the unique horrors of wartime Ukraine.

A ndrei Romanovich Chikatilo was born on October 16, 1936 in Yablochnoye, Ukraine. It was a tough time and place in which to enter the world. Ukraine had suffered terribly from Stalin's policies of agricultural collectivization (consolidating individual farms into units to produce food for the growing urban classes) and political persecution. Famine was endemic. In fact, Chikatilo's mother had told him that his elder brother, Steppan, had actually been killed and cannibalized by neighbors during the early years of the war.

In 1941, Germany invaded the Soviet Union, and the reign of terror unleashed by the Nazis

◄ Andrei Chikatilo, here seen during his trial in 1992. He was held in the courtroom in a steel cage, to protect him from enraged relatives of his victims.

spread deep into Ukraine. Left alone with his mother—Chikatilo's father had been conscripted into the armed forces—the young boy was initially fearful of what he saw around him. He became a regular bedwetter, for which he was severely punished. He also became intimately familiar

▼ A photograph of unidentified young female who became one of Andrei Chikatilo's murder victims. Chikatilo preyed on vulnerable individuals on the margins of Soviet society.

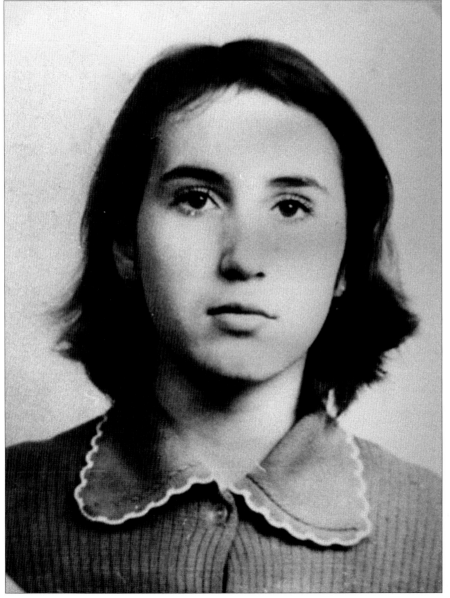

with scenes of death and destruction caused by German bombing raids, sights that began to hold something of an appeal for the disturbed young man. Eventually his father came home from the war in 1949. Having been captured by the Germans and held as a prisoner of war, his father was subsequently branded a traitor by the Soviet authorities.

It is little wonder that Chikatilo continued to show disturbing personal traits even after the war ended in 1945. Academically, he seemed bright and held a possible future in the legal profession. Yet having failed the entrance exam to Moscow State University, he then undertook his mandatory military service before becoming a telephone engineer in 1960.

Chikatilo was an unsettled character, plagued by sexual impotence following a disastrous encounter with a woman, who spread the story throughout their group of friends. She would have no idea of the enmity Chikatilo would develop toward women on account of this incident, or what it would lead to.

Despite this experience, in 1963 Chikatilo married. The union produced two children, although it appears that the method of conception involved masturbation and the manual insertion of semen. It seemed as if marriage might put Chikatilo on

Timeline of a Murder

1: Friday December 22, 1978. After a day at work, Andrei Chikatilo heads out around the streets of Shakhty, a city in the Rostov Oblast, northwest of Rostov-on-Don. He begins to watch the people who come and go on the streets as night falls.

2: It is already dark when he spots a young girl, nine-year-old *Yelena Zakotnova*, waiting at a tram stop on the city streets, heading home after playing with a friend. She is wearing a red coat and a fur hat to protect her against the cold.

3: Chikatilo crosses the street and strikes up a conversation with Yelena. To the young girl he seems friendly and unthreatening. She confesses that she badly needs the bathroom, and Chikatilo offers to take her to his nearby house—actually little more than a wooden hut—on nearby Mezhevoi Pereulok lane.

4: Yelena goes with Chikatilo. As soon as they enter the house, Chikatilo launches a frantic attack on Yelena, ripping off her clothes and attempting to rape her. During this phase of the attack he makes Yelena bleed, a sight that whips him into a frenzy. He pulls out a knife and stabs her repeatedly.

5: In a few horrifying minutes, Yelena is dead. Chikatilo waits a few hours then carries the dead girl plus her clothes and schoolbag down to the Grushevka River and disposes of them. The girl and her clothes go into the river, but Chikatilo throws the bag too hard and it is lost on the opposite bank.

6: Chikatilo heads back to the school at which he worked and cleans himself up. He then goes home before his wife returns from work.

▲ Psychiatrist Alexander Bukhanovsky looks through Chikatilo's case files. Bukhanovsky prepared a detailed psychological profile for Chikatilo's trial in 1992, and was important in prompting Chikatilo's confessions.

▲ The dirt path running through a wooded area in Aviators' Park where the bodies of two of Andrei Chikatilo's murder victims of were found, both horribly mutilated.

the right track. In 1971 he completed a correspondence degree in Russian literature, and began a career teaching in a local school. Yet accusations steadily emerged that Chikatilo was molesting students, both male and female—in one incident he marched into a girls' dormitory in his underwear, and stood there masturbating. Had he stopped at merely grotesque displays of his warped sexuality, his evil might have been contained.

PREYING ON THE WEAK

On December 22, 1978, Chikatilo met a nine-year-old girl, Yelena Zakotnova, outside the shack he had purchased on the edge of town. The shack was essentially a lair, a place in which he could indulge his fantasies away from the eyes of his family. Yelena was simply playing in the street, and when she needed the bathroom Chikatilo seized his chance. He led her inside, and immediately began a violent sexual assault that set the scene for more than a decade of killing. Chikatilo suffered from impotence and sexual dysfunction, but while pulling the girl's clothes off he drew blood—and experienced an immediate erection in response. Following the dark logic of his own body, Chikatilo then began repeatedly stabbing Yelena with a knife in a masturbatory action, the killing of the unfortunate girl being the vehicle for his orgasm. His purpose achieved, Chikatilo then simply threw the body into a river, where it was discovered by police two days later.

It's hard to believe that Cold War ideology can enter into a serial killer investigation, but such is exactly what occurred in the case of Chikatilo. According to contemporary communist thinking, the serial-killer phenomenon was a product of capitalist societies, a mental aberration brought about by iniquitous labor conditions and the dislocation of the individual from his or her true self. For the early years of his reign of terror, Chikatilo benefited from this outlook, as local police often treated each death on an individual basis, rather than connecting the dots. Such was certainly the case with the murder of Yelena Zakotnova. Despite blood having been found outside Chikatilo's shack, about which he was questioned, the Soviet police instead arrested a local sex offender, who was subsequently convicted and executed for the crime.

Chikatilo then went through a series of teaching positions, before finally being muscled out of education altogether. He next found work as a factory supply clerk in Rostovnerud, a job that provided opportunities for Chikatilo to travel around and select his next victims—always from the poor and disadvantaged underclass—with greater facility. After the murder of Yelena Zakotnova, Chikatilo would wait nearly two years before his next killing (as far as we know). On September 3, 1981, Chikatilo met 17-year-old boarding school student Larisa Tkachenko. The promise of a drink caused Larisa to drop her guard, even as Chikatilo led her on a shortcut through some local woods. He attacked her there with utter brutality, throttling her to death before ejaculating on and dancing around her corpse.

PATHOLOGY OF A SERIAL KILLER

The murder of Larisa Tkachenko was essentially the true beginning of Chikatilo's predations. In 1982 he would kill seven people, and eight the following year. In 1984 he killed 15 times. Most of his victims were young, ranging from the age of eight

▼ A chilling piece of evidence—a close-up view of a black leather bag owned by Andrei Chikatilo. Chikatilo used the bag to carry knives, rope, and, on occasions, his victims' body parts.

(Alexander Dyakonov in 1989, his youngest victim) to their late teens, but he also killed a number of women who were in their 20s, 30s, and 40s. (His oldest victim was Marta Ryabenko, 45, killed in Aviators' Park in Rostov on February 21, 1984.) Moreover, the manner of killing became increasingly, horrifyingly psychotic. Chikatilo would often tie up his prey, and then inflict terrible mutilations upon them with a knife or just his teeth and bare hands. He would bite off the nose or genitals, rip open the belly with his nails, or stab the victim multiple times. There was often a cannibalistic element to the violence—he would eat external and internal body parts, expressing a particular fondness for consuming the uterus of female victims. Sometimes the victims would still be alive, depending on what had been removed, while watching him eat. The attacks were crazed, monstrous affairs, and it is impossible to imagine the terror of those who had died under these attacks.

ACCEPTANCE

By September 1983, the Rostov police had so many bodies killed in a similar fashion they could no longer deny that they had a serial killer in their midst. Incredibly, it actually took the local communist party officials almost another year to publicly accept the same conclusion, by which time Chikatilo had

Timeline of a Murderer—Chikatilo's 53 Known Victims

NUMBER	DATE	VICTIM	AGE
1	December 22, 1978	Yelena Zakotnova	9
2	September 3, 1981	Larisa Tkachenko	17
3	June 12, 1982	Lyubov Biryuk	13
4	July 25, 1982	Lyubov Volobuyeva	14
5	August 13, 1982	Oleg Pozhidayev	9
6	August 16, 1982	Olga Kuprina	16
7	September 8, 1982	Irina Karabelnikova	19
8	September 15, 1982	Sergei Kuzmin	15
9	December 11, 1982	Olga Stalmachenok	10
10	After June 18, 1983	Laura Sarkisyan	15
11	July 1983	Irina Dunenkova	13
12	July 1983	Lyudmila Kushuba	24
13	August 9, 1983	Igor Gudkov	7
14	After September 19, 1983	Valentina Chuchulina	22
15	Summer or fall 1983	Unknown woman	18–25
16	October 27, 1983	Vera Shevkun	19
17	December 27, 1983	Sergei Markov	14
18	January 9, 1984	Natalya Shalapinina	17
19	February 21, 1984	Marta Ryabenko	45
20	March 24, 1984	Dmitry Ptashnikov	10
21	May 25, 1984	Tatyana Petrosyan	32
22	May 25, 1984	Svetlana Petrosyan	11
23	June 1984	Yelena Bakulina	22
24	July 10, 1984	Dmitry Illarionov	13
25	July 19, 1984	Anna Lemesheva	19
26	July 1984	Svetlana Tsana	20
27	August 2, 1984	Natalya Golosovskaya	16

murdered 30 people. Eventually a police unit from Moscow, headed by Major Mikhail Fetisov, was sent to Rostov to investigate the murders. The team included a forensic analyst, Victor Burakov, who had ventured into the largely unfamiliar waters of investigating a major serial killer.

Priority individuals for investigation were the obvious candidates—mentally disturbed people, pedophiles, and other sex offenders—but indicative of contemporary thinking they also included homosexuals. The investigatory techniques used could be brutally persuasive—police interrogations often extracted confessions from the suspects, which were then rendered worthless by either more substantial police work or by the appearance of another body.

A break came on September 14, 1984. Undercover police operating in a Rostov market observed Chikatilo attempting to pick up young women. He was stopped and searched, and his briefcase contained a hefty knife, a length of rope, and a container of Vaseline. His description also matched that of a man seen talking to 10-year-old Dmitry Ptashnikov, who had been abducted and murdered on March 24, 1984. Chikatilo was taken into custody. Tragically, the police did not have the records of Chikatilo's previous sexual misbehaviors. Furthermore, although he fitted the description of

NUMBER	DATE	VICTIM	AGE
28	August 7, 1984	Lyudmila Alekseyeva	17
29	August 8–11, 1984	Unknown woman	20–25
30	August 13, 1984	Akmaral Seydaliyeva	12
31	August 28, 1984	Alexander Chepel	11
32	September 6, 1984	Irina Luchinskaya	24
33	July 31, 1985	Natalya Pokhlistova	18
34	August 25, 1985	Irina Gulyayeva	18
35	May 16, 1987	Oleg Makarenkov	13
36	July 29, 1987	Ivan Bilovetsky	12
37	September 15, 1987	Yuri Tereshonok	16
38	April 1–4, 1988	Unknown woman	18–25
39	May 15, 1988	Alexei Voronko	9
40	July 14, 1988	Yevgeny Muratov	15
41	March 8, 1989	Tatyana Ryzhova	16
42	May 11, 1989	Alexander Dyakonov	8
43	June 20, 1989	Alexei Moiseyev	10
44	August 19, 1989	Helena Varga	19
45	August 28, 1989	Alexei Khobotov	10
46	January 14, 1990	Andrei Kravchenko	11
47	March 7, 1990	Yaroslav Makarov	10
48	April 4, 1990	Lyubov Zuyeva	31
49	July 28, 1990	Viktor Petrov	13
50	August 14, 1990	Ivan Fomin	11
51	October 16, 1990	Vadim Gromov	16
52	October 30, 1990	Viktor Tishchenko	16
53	November 6, 1990	Svetlana Korostik	22

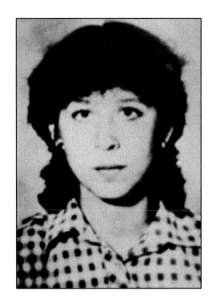

▲ Portraits of four young female murder victims of Andrei Chikatilo. Chikatilo's victims were almost exclusively women, girls, or young boys—adult males held little interest for him.

thing the police could pin on Chikatilo was an outstanding charge for theft from a former employer. He was convicted of this minor charge and was sentenced to a year in prison, but he only served three months and was released in December 1984.

FINAL ARREST
Once released from prison, Chikatilo actually kept something of a low profile for many months, only resuming killing in August 1985. But once he began murdering again, he did so with typical enthusiasm. By August 1989, he had murdered another 11 people in his ghastly style, although his run-in with the law had made him a little more circumspect. For example, he began committing most of his murders well away from the Rostov area, taking advantage of the travel that was part and parcel of his job.

Yet steadily the police professionalized their operation to catch this monster, even bringing in a forensic psychiatrist to create a psychological profile of the killer. They slowly built up a picture of the type of man they were looking for, and also mapped out the murder locations to see if a pattern emerged. By 1990, for example, it became clear that many of the killings, or at least body disposals, occurred around train or bus stations, and these locations were put under heavy surveillance.

Furthermore, Chikatilo himself was back under suspicion. On November 6, 1990, he was stopped and questioned by a policeman after he was caught

the man related to the Ptashnikov murder, his blood type tested as Group A—semen samples from Ptashnikov indicated an AB blood type. In rare cases an individual's blood type can vary according to the part of the body from which the sample is taken. Unfortunately for more than two dozen other victims, Chikatilo was one of these cases. The only

emerging from some woodland, having just killed and mutilated 22-year-old Svetlana Korostik. Despite his suspicious appearance, Chikatilo was not arrested—his briefcase, which contained Korostik's severed breasts, was obviously not searched. Yet his name went on record, and when Korostik's body was discovered a week later officers were able to connect Chikatilo with the murder.

On November 20, 1990, having killed 53 people (three of whom were never found), Chikatilo was finally arrested. It would take 10 days of subtle questioning before Chikatilo confessed to his litany of dreadful crimes—he revealed 20 more murders than the police were actually investigating. A sperm sample tested for the AB group, corroborating earlier forensic evidence. The police now had their serial killer.

TRIAL AND EXECUTION

The trial of Andrei Chikatilo began in April 1992, by which time the Soviet Union had ceased to exist. It was an emotionally charged trial; Chikatilo was locked inside a cage in the courtroom to protect him from the vengeance of distressed relatives of the murder victims. Chikatilo himself presented a picture of dark insanity, on two occasions exposing his genitals to the court. He delivered rambling speeches full of incoherent political and social comment, but also revealed some of the horrors of his childhood, and admitted "I am a freak of nature, a mad beast."

In October 1992, Chikatilo was found guilty of 52 murders, and received a death sentence for each. He spent just over a year on death row before, on February 14, 1994, he was executed by a single gunshot to the head in a soundproof room in Novocherkassk prison. In death he was given the easy journey he denied to dozens of his victims.

▼ Chikatilo in captivity, 1992. During his trial he exhibited a clear psychosis, regularly exposing himself, singing, and refusing to answer questions.

JOHN WAYNE GACY

John Wayne Gacy presents the classic dual personality of many of serial killers. In public, he wore an affable and engaging persona, even working as a children's entertainer. Behind closed doors, however, he had a predilection for raping and murdering young men, killing 33 people before justice finally caught up with him.

If there ever was a childhood designed to produce a disturbed young man, then John Wayne Gacy's was it. He was born on March 17, 1942 in Chicago, Illinois. While outwardly a normal Roman Catholic family, within the home there was the tension of a violent and abusive father. John, one of three children, began to receive beatings at the age of four, and shortly afterward started suffering from epileptic seizures. His new

◄ Police officers and firefighters remove one of more than two dozen murder victims found in the crawl space of John Wayne Gacy's home in Norwood Park Township, Des Plaines, Illinois.

▲ Some 5000 demonstrators gathered on May 9, 1994 to support the scheduled execution of John Wayne Gacy. They got their wish—Gacy died by lethal injection the following day.

medical condition did not stop the abuse, and at the age of six his father even shot John's dog as punishment for some minor infraction. From around the age of seven, there were also signs of a confused sexuality developing in the young boy. He stole his mother's underwear on several occasions, and was either beaten or forced to wear the underwear to school as punishment. He also suffered at the hands of other people, being sexually abused by a building contractor friend of his father at the age of nine.

His obsession with female underwear continued, and early attempts to strike up relationships with girls tended to be disastrous. Nevertheless, by the age of 18 he seemed to be sorting himself out, working in local politics for the Democratic Party and engaging in voluntary service. Appearances were deceptive, however. In 1961 he entered the medical profession, first as an ambulance driver in Las Vegas, then as a mortuary attendant. The latter employment did him no good at all. He became fixated with the dead bodies, stripping them and conducting minor experiments on them. Gacy even acquired something of a taste for climbing in and out of mortuary caskets. It was little wonder that his activities soon came to official attention, and he was fired from his post.

CAREER AND MARRIAGE

Following his experience in Las Vegas, life seemed to pick up a little for John Wayne Gacy. Having graduated from Northwestern Business College, back in Chicago, in 1962, he then did well, working

Timeline of a Murder

1: December 11, 1978. Fifteen-year-old *Robert Piest* is working in the local Nisson Pharmacy in Des Plaines, Illinois. He has about an hour left before he finishes his shift.

2: PDM Contractors, John Wayne Gacy's building company, is also doing work on the pharmacy premises. He approaches Piest and offers him construction work. In the process of saving for a car, Piest accepts the offer of work.

3: Piest is last seen talking to Gacy outside the shop in the early evening. He's never seen alive again. By 11:30 P.M.

the Piest family have contacted the police, concerned because the boy has not come home for his mother's birthday party.

4: Details are unclear, but it appears that Gacy took Piest back to his house, where he assaulted and asphyxiated him. He then threw Piest's body in the Illinois River.

5: April 1979. Piest's remains are recovered from the Illinois River, by which time Gacy has been arrested for numerous other murders.

as a salesman for Nunn Bush Shores. He also struck up a relationship with one Marlynn Myers, whom he married in 1964. They moved to Waterloo, Iowa, the same year, where John managed three Kentucky Fried Chicken branches owned by Marlynn's father. John and Marlynn both became extremely active in local community work, and seemed to be pillars of the community, Gacy involving himself heavily with the U.S. Junior Chapter (Jaycees) organization. Furthermore, in 1966 and 1967 Marlynn gave birth to two children, a son, Michael, and a daughter, Christine.

Yet Gacy had something of a hidden life. In 1964, shortly before he got married, he had a homosexual encounter with a man, and in 1967 what might have been a hidden, but ultimately acceptable, sexuality turned into something else. He began a series of forcible or consensual sexual relationships with 16-year-old boys in the local

▼ Police and forensic units gather outside Gacy's home in Des Plaines, Illinois. Gacy's tendency to kill and bury at the same location is not uncommon among predatory serial killers.

▲ John Wayne Gacy seen here on his wedding day with second wife Carole Hoff, June 1972. Within three years Carole would ask for a divorce, promoted in part by Gacy's addiction to homosexual pornography.

community, two of whom told the police. Gacy was charged with the rape of one of his young employees, Mark Miller, in 1968, for which he received a sentence of 10 years' imprisonment and was ordered to undertake psychiatric evaluation.

Although Gacy was paroled after 18 months in prison, his life truly started to unravel. His wife left him, taking the two children with her, and his father died while he was in prison. He went to live with his mother in Chicago, but old habits died hard, and he was charged with the attempted rape of a teen in 1971. He escaped this charge when the plaintiff failed to turn up for the court hearing. Remarkably, he struck up another relationship, this time with divorcée Carole Hoff, whom he married on June 1, 1972. Hoff believe that the jovial Gacy was a reformed character. If she'd known what he was really doing in his spare time, she would have fled.

ON A ROLL

John Wayne Gacy crossed the line from assault to murder on January 3, 1972. On that day, Gacy propositioned a 15-year-old boy, Timothy McCoy,

while posing as a police officer. (He would often use the name Detective Jack Hanley, an officer whom he had met during his brushes with the law in 1969.) The boy resisted his advances, and in response Gacy stabbed him to death, and stuffed the body in the crawl space beneath his house. Just four days later he turned violent again, clubbing a 24-year-old man who had refused to perform oral sex on him. For this offence he was arrested, but the charges were dropped when he filed a counter-charge.

For the next three years Gacy seemed to stay out of trouble, at least in terms of his sexual relations. He suffered a stroke in 1973, however, and the quality of his marriage took a significant downturn when he stopped having sexual relations with Carole. The critical year was 1975. Carole asked him for a divorce, a response not only to their barren love life, but also to the discovery that he had continued to have homosexual encounters, and was in possession of large amounts of homosexual pornography. Weirdly, these events occurred roughly at the same time as he created the character of PoGo the clown, and began performing at children's parties in his spare time.

With his marriage over, Gacy now began to kill with terrifying regularity. His second victim, on July 31, 1975, was 17-year-old John Butkovich, whom he strangled, and buried the body under his garage. The following year he murdered no fewer than nine times, most of the bodies, as with previous victims, going in the crawl space of the house. By the end of the year, Gacy was becoming an expert murderer,

and had developed a very clear strategy of deceit and killing. First he would target his young male victims, selected from either the streets or among the workforce of his building company. (He would often hire men to whom he was attracted specifically with the expectation of murdering them.) Gacy would then take them back to his house, where he gave them alcohol and drugs and offered to show them one of the magic tricks he

▼ November 1998. Chicago police begin excavating around the apartment building where Gacy's mother used to live. The grid lines in the the garden help make the search more methodical.

performed. He thereby was able to handcuff the victim, whereupon he proceeded to assault, rape, and then strangle him. No unusual torture was used, and Gacy's sexuality seems confused, as Brian Lane and Winifred Gregg have pointed out in their *Encyclopedia of Serial Killers* (Berkeley, 1995): "Curiously, Gacy always claimed that he was not a homosexual, and that indeed he hated homosexuals—a fact which, if true, would account in part for the conscience-free way in which he could kill his sex partners (even though they were themselves not homosexual)."

Gacy would murder a total of 14 more men in 1977–78. Amid this efficiency, however, he also made some mistakes. On March 21, 1978, he abducted, chloroformed, and raped a young man called Jeffrey Rignall, but then simply left him in a local park rather than killing him. Rignall went to the police,

Timeline of a Murderer—Gacy's Identified Victims

DATE	VICTIM	AGE	DETAILS
January 3, 1972	Timothy McCoy	9	A Greyhound bus boy, stabbed to death and buried in the crawl space of Gacy's home.
July 31, 1975	John Butkovich	17	Also known as "Little John."
April 6, 1976	Darrell Sampson	18	Disappears; later found buried in the crawl space.
May 14, 1976	Randall Reffett	15	Killed on the same day as Sam Stapleton.
May 14, 1976	Sam Stapleton	14	Killed on the same day as Randall Reffett, one of only two occasions, as far as we know, that Gacy murdered twice on the same day.
June 3, 1976	Michael Bonnin	17	
June 13, 1976	William Carroll	16	
August 6, 1976	Rick Johnston	17	Murdered after he disappeared following a rock concert.
October 25, 1976	Kenneth Parker	16	
October 25, 1976	Michael Marino	14	Killed on the same day as Kenneth Parker.
December 12, 1976	Gregory Godzik	17	
January 20, 1977	John Szyc	19	A street hustler who disappeared after contact with Gacy.
March 15, 1977	Jon Prestidge	20	
July 5, 1977	Matthew Bowman	19	
September 15, 1977	Robert Gilroy	18	Reported missing when he failed to show up for his horse-riding meeting.
September 25, 1977	John Mowery	19	
October 17, 1977	Russell Nelson	21	Along with James Mazzara, Gacy's oldest victim.
November 10, 1977	Robert Winch	16	
November 18, 1977	Tommy Boling	20	
December 9, 1977	David Talsma	19	
February 16, 1978	William Kindred	19	
June 1978	Timothy O'Rourke	20	
November 4, 1978	Frank Landingin	19	Around this time Gacy begins disposing of bodies in a nearby river, the crawl space under his house being full.
November 24, 1978	James Mazzara	21	
December 11, 1978	Robert Piest	15	The investigation of Piest's murder eventually leads to Gacy's arrest.

who rejected the charges, but Rignall managed to press a successful civil prosecution, which was settled out of court in September upon the payment of a fine.

SUSPICION

Gacy's undoing was the murder of his final victim, 15-year-old Robert Piest, on December 11, 1978. Piest was last seen in Gacy's company, and when his disappearance was reported the police eventually obtained a search warrant for Gacy's house. On their initial visit they found pornography and drugs. On a subsequent visit a few days later, however, they searched the crawl space underneath his house, led there partly by the dreadful smell they had detected. Underneath his house and underneath the garage, they found a total of 28 bodies.

Gacy quickly came clean, and in December 1978 he confessed to the murder of 33 people. Later,

during his trial, he attempted to portray himself as a split personality, an insane individual not in control of his actions. The jury, however, did not believe this fabrication, and in March 1980 he was sentenced to no fewer than 12 death sentences and 21 life sentences.

Gacy appealed furiously against his sentences, but was denied his final appeal by the U.S. Supreme Court in March 1985. Bizarrely, during his time on death row he actually made something of a living by painting and selling clown pictures, and even by charging for signed photographs of himself. His time finally ran out on May 10, 1994, when he was executed by lethal injection, his last words reportedly being "Kiss my ass."

▼ One of Gacy's unnerving post-incarceration paintings—the self-portrait "Pogo the Clown." He sold such paintings while on death row.

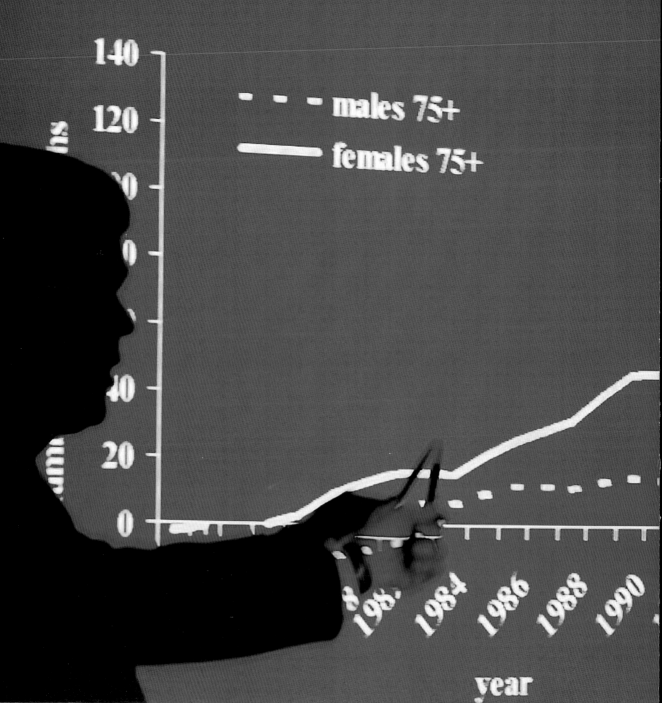

among Shipman's
remises, aged 75

1994 1996 1998

HAROLD SHIPMAN

On June 24, 1998, Angela Woodruff received a call from her mother's family doctor in Hyde, UK, telling her that her mother had suddenly died. Little did she realize at the time, but as she worked through her grief over the next few weeks, her suspicions would begin to unmask one of the most prolific serial killers in history.

It came as the most profound shock to Angela Woodruff when Dr. Harold Shipman's call came through. Although former mayoress Kathleen Grundy was 81 years old, she had appeared to be in robust good health, indicated by her constant dedication to local charity work. Nevertheless, Shipman told her that there would be no need for a postmortem, as he had been by to see her only a few hours earlier to acquire blood

◄ An academic presentation on the Harold Shipman case makes a graphic illustration of Shipman's murderous career as a medical doctor, the number of killings intensifying in the late 1990s.

◄ Dr. Harold Shipman photographed in Hyde, Greater Manchester, as he came under the police spotlight in 1998. Shipman's grandfatherly demeanor was a key reason why he fell beyond suspicion for so long.

samples. Having herself known Dr. Shipman for many years, Angela simply trusted that there was no foul play.

Events became more suspicious, however, in the days following Kathleen's funeral. A firm of lawyers contacted Angela regarding Kathleen's will—this in itself came as a surprise to Angela, as she was a lawyer and her own firm had drawn up Kathleen's will in 1986. When she received a copy of the new will two things struck her. First, it was a forgery, and second, Dr. Harold Shipman was named as the beneficiary of £386,000 (nearly $600,000). Beginning to fear the worst, she

contacted the Hyde police, who exhumed the body of Kathleen Grundy and conducted a full postmortem. The examination showed Kathleen Grundy had died from an overdose of morphine. A search of Shipman's house revealed the typewriter on which the fake will had been written.

The Hyde police now had clear evidence with which to charge Harold Shipman with murder. Yet the case was about to expand into realms that neither the police nor the public could have ever foreseen.

DISTANT CHARACTER

Harold Shipman was born on June 14, 1946. His early life was dominated by a powerful and

▼ Shipman's office on Market Street, in Hyde, Greater Manchester. Victims were killed both in his office and in their own homes.

Timeline of a Murderer—Unlawful Killings/Confirmed Victims of Harold Shipman

NB: This list is not exhaustive, and there are numerous other deaths held as suspicious.

1975
March 17: Eva Lyons, 70.

1978
August 7: Sarah Hannah Marsland, 86.
August 30: Mary Ellen Jordan, 73.
December 7: Harold Bramwell, 73.
December 20: Annie Campbell, 88.

1979
August 10: Alice Maude Gorton, 76.
November 28:
   Jack Leslie Shelmerdine, 77.

1981
April 18: May Slater, 84.
August 26: Elizabeth Ashworth, 81.

1983
January 4: Percy Ward, 90.
June 28: Moira Ashton Fox, 77.

1984
January 7: Dorothy Tucker, 51.
February 8: Gladys Roberts, 78.
April 15: Joseph Bardsley, 83.
April 24: Winifred Arrowsmith, 70.
September 21:
   Mary Winterbottom, 76.
November 27: Ada Ashworth, 87.
December 17:
   Joseph Vincent Everall, 80.
December 18: Edith Wibberley, 76.
December 24: Eileen Theresa Cox, 72.

1985
January 2: Peter Lewis, 41.
February 1: May Brookes, 74.
February 4: Ellen Higson, 84.
February 15:
   Margaret Ann Conway, 69.
February 22: Kathleen McDonald, 73.
June 26: Thomas Moult, 70.
June 26: Mildred Robinson, 84.
August 23:
   Frances Elizabeth Turner, 85.
December 17: Selina Mackenzie, 77.
December 20: Vera Bramwell, 79.
December 31: Fred Kellett, 79.

1986
January 7: Deborah Middleton, 81.
April 23: Dorothy Fletcher, 74.
June 6: Thomas Fowden, 81.
September 15:
   Mona Ashton White, 63.
October 7: Mary Tomlin, 73.
November 17: Beatrice Toft, 59.
December 16: Lily Broadbent, 75.
December 23: James Wood, 82.

1987
March 30: Frank Halliday, 76.
April 1: Albert Cheetham, 85.
April 16: Alice Thomas, 83.
May 8: Jane Frances Rostron, 78.
September 14: Nancy Anne
   Brassington, 71.
December 11: Margaret Townsend,
   80.
December 29: Nellie Bardsley, 69.
December 30: Elizabeth Ann Rogers,
   74.

1988
January 5: Elizabeth Fletcher, 90.
January 15: Alice Mary Jones, 83.
February 9:
   Dorothea Hill Renwick, 90.
February 15: Ann Cooper, 93.
February 15: Jane Jones, 83.
February 16: Lavinia Robinson, 84.
September 18: Rose Ann Adshead, 80.
October 20: Alice Prestwich, 69.
November 6: Walter Tingle, 85.
December 17: Harry Stafford, 87.
December 19: Ethel Bennett, 80.

1989
January 31: Wilfred Chappell, 80.
March 8: Mary Emma Hamer, 81.
May 12: Beatrice Helen Clee, 78.
June 5: Josephine Hall, 69.
July 6: Hilda Fitton, 75.
August 14: Marion Carradice, 80.
September 22: Elsie Harrop, 82.
September 26: Elizabeth M. Burke, 82.
October 15:
   Sarah Jane Williamson, 82.

1989 (continued)
October 16: John Charlton, 81.
October 18:
   George Edgar Vizor, 67.
November 6:
   Joseph Frank Wilcockson, 85.

1990
September 18: Dorothy Rowarth, 56.
December 30: Mary Rose Dudley, 69.

1992
October 7: Monica Rene Sparkes, 72.

1993
February 24: Hilda Mary Couzens, 92.
February 24: Olive Heginbotham, 86.
March 22: Amy Whitehead, 82.
April 8: Mary Emma Andrew, 86.
April 17: Sarah Ashworth, 74.
April 29: Marjorie Parker, 74.
May 2: Nellie Mullen, 77.
May 4: Edna May Llewellyn, 68.
May 12: Emily Morgan, 84.
May 13: Violet May Bird, 60.
July 22:
   Jose Kathleen Diana Richards, 74.
August 16: Edith Calverley, 77.
December 16: Joseph Leigh, 78.
December 22: Eileen Robinson, 54.
December 31:
   Charles Edward Brocklehurst, 90.

1994
January 4: Joan Milray Harding, 82.
January 13: Christine Hancock, 53.
February 9: Elsie Platt, 73.
May 17: Mary Alice Smith, 84.
May 25: Ronnie Devenport, 57.
June 15: Cicely Sharples, 87.
June 17: Alice Christine Kitchen, 70.
July 27: Maria Thornton, 78.
November 25: Henrietta Walker, 87.
November 30:
   Elizabeth Ellen Mellor, 75.
December 29:
   John Bennett Molesdale, 81.

1995
January 9: Alice Kennedy, 88.
March 1: Lucy Virgin, 70.
March 7: Netta Ashcroft, 71.
March 7: Lily Bardsley, 88.
March 13:
    Marie Antoinette Fernley, 53.
March 21: John Crompton, 82.
March 26: Frank Crompton, 86.
March 31: Vera Brocklehurst, 70.
April 10:
    Angela Philomena Tierney, 71.
April 13: Edith Scott, 85.
April 14: Clara Hackney, 84.
April 21:
    Renate Eldtraude Overton, 47.
May 4: Kate Maud Sellors, 75.
June 2: Clifford Barnes Heapey, 85.
June 13: Bertha Moss, 68.
June 17: Brenda Ashworth, 63.
June 29: Ernest Rudol, 82.
July 12: Ada Matley Hilton, 88.
July 31: Irene Aitken, 65.
August 29:
    Arthur Henderson Stopford, 82.
September 14: Geoffrey Bogle, 72.
September 26:
    Dora Elizabeth Ashton, 87.
October 24:
    Muriel Margaret Ward, 87.
November 8: Edith Brock, 74.
November 22:
    Charles Henry Barlow, 88.
November 25:
    Konrad Peter Ovcar-Robinson, 43.
December 14:
    Elizabeth Teresa Sigley, 67.
December 14:
    Kenneth Wharmby Woodhead, 75.

1996
January 2: Hilda Mary Hibbert, 81.
January 11: Erla Copeland, 79.
February 21:
    Jane Elizabeth Shelmerdine, 80.
February 27:
    John Sheard Greenhalgh, 88.
March 12:
    Minnie Doris Irene Galpin, 71.

1996 (continued)
April 18: Marjorie Hope Waller, 79.
April 24: John Stone, 77.
May 7: Elsie Godfrey, 85.
May 13: Edith Brady, 72.
May 29: Valerie Cuthbert, 54.
May 30: Lilian Cullen, 77.
June 6: Renee Lacey, 63.
June 10: Leah Fogg, 82.
June 17: Gladys Saunders, 82.
June 25: Nellie Bennett, 86.
June 25: Margaret Mary Vickers, 81.
July 2: Tom Balfour Russell, 77.
July 11: Irene Turner, 67.
July 16: Carrie Leigh, 81.
July 19: Marion Elizabeth Higham, 84.
July 24: Elsie Hannible, 85.
July 29: Elsie Barker, 84.
August 30: Sidney Arthur Smith, 76.
September12:
    Dorothy Mary Andrew, 85.
September 20: Anne Lilian Ralphs, 75.
October 23: Millicent Garside, 76.
November 20: Irene Heathcote, 76.
November 23: Samuel Mills, 89.
December 4: Thomas Cheetham, 78.
December 17:
    Kenneth Ernest Smith, 73.

1997
January 2: Eileen Daphne Crompton.
January 3: David Alan Harrison, 47.
January 8: Elsie Lorna Dean, 69.
January 20: Irene Brooder, 76.
January 27: Charlotte Bennison, 89.
February 3: Charles Henry Killan, 90.
February 4: Betty Royston, 70.
February 23: Joyce Woodhead, 74.
February 28: Lizzie Adams, 77.
March 22: Rose Garlick, 76.
March 27: May Lowe, 84.
April 21: Mary Coutts, 80.
April 25: Elsie Cheetham, 76.
April 25: Jean Lilley, 58.
May 2: Lena Norah Slater, 68.
May 12: Ethel May Kellet, 74.
May 21: Doris Earls, 79.
May 29: Ivy Lomas, 63.
June 24: Vera Whittingslow, 69.

1997 (continued)
July 7: Maureen Lamonnier Jackson, 51.
July 14: Muriel Grimshaw, 76.
July 25: John Louden Livesey, 69.
July 28: Lily Newby Taylor, 86.
August 10:
    Dorothy Doretta Hopkins, 72.
September 1: Nancy Jackson, 81.
September 22: Mavis Mary Pickup, 79.
September 26: Bessie Swann, 79.
September 29: Enid Otter, 77.
November 10: Florence Lewis, 79.
November 14: Mary Walls, 78.
November 21:
    Elizabeth Mary Baddeley, 83.
November 24: Marie Quinn, 67.
December 8: Elizabeth Battersby, 70.
December 9:
    Laura Kathleen Wagstaff, 81.
December 10: Bianka Pomfret, 49.
December 18: Alice Black, 73.
December 24: James Joseph King, 83.

1998
January 22: Mabel Shawcross, 79.
January 26: Norah Nuttall, 64.
February 2: Cissie Davies, 73.
February 9: Pamela Marguerite Hillier, 68.
February 13: Laura Frances Linn, 83.
February 15: Irene Berry, 74.
February 18: Maureen Alice Ward, 57.
February 27: Joan Edwina Dean, 75.
March 4: Harold Eddleston, 77.
March 6: Margaret Anne Waldron, 65.
March 7: Irene Chapman, 74.
March 13: Dorothy Long.
March 17: Lily Higgins, 83.
20 March 20: Ada Warburton, 77.
March 24: Martha Marley, 88.
May 11: Winifred Mellor, 73.
June 12: Joan May Melia, 73.
June 24: Kathleen Grundy, 81.

◄ Hundreds of friends and relatives of victims of Harold Shipman gathered together for a special ecumenical service of prayer at St George's Church in Hyde, Greater Manchester, in July 2002. A bell tolled 215 times—one for each victim—in a moving tribute to Harold Shipman's victims and their families.

controlling mother, Vera, who oversaw every aspect of his life from his relationships to his clothing. Vera instilled in Harold a strong sense his own superiority, which was returned by Harold's complete devotion to his mother. Cancer eventually robbed Harold of his mother in June 1963, the teenage boy having watched her deterioration with great distress. One abiding memory of her illness, however, was how injections of morphine from her family doctor would bring instant relief to her suffering. He would later draw on this memory to perform more than 200 murders.

Yet his history of killing was in the future at this point. As a young adult he attended Leeds University medical school, in which most of his fellow medical students saw him as a strange and distant character. He did make one connection, with a 17-year-old local girl called Primrose (not a student), whom he married in his first year of studies when she became pregnant.

Shipman graduated from medical school in 1970. His first job was as a junior houseman at Pontefract General Infirmary in West Yorkshire, before going on to General Practice in Todmorden, also in Yorkshire. It was while working in the local doctor's office in Todmorden that Shipman developed some bad habits. He began injecting himself with pethidine (a painkiller, usually used to treat labor pains, to which he was addicted), which he illegally obtained by signing false prescriptions for his patients. His deceit and addiction were eventually discovered by the office, whose partners were naturally now keen to get rid of Shipman. Although he found himself temporarily without a job, and had been convicted and fined £600 (about $930) for drugs and fraud offences, Shipman was not struck off the medical register. He was free to take another job, and in 1979 he began working as a General Practitioner (GP) in the Doneybrooke Medical Centre in Hyde, Greater Manchester.

MEDICAL MURDER

Although Shipman informed his new employers of his troubled past, to them it seemed as if he was a reformed character. He had four children by this time, and he quickly struck up a good rapport with the many elderly people who frequented the office. Indeed, it would be an irony of Harold Shipman's life that many of his patients would remain fiercely loyal to his reputation even when the evidence of his crimes became overwhelming.

It is unclear when Harold Shipman began killing people. The individuals listed in the timeline here are just those classified as the victims of unlawful killing; there are many others that remain as suspicious cases. Yet even in the two

Timeline of a Murder

1: November 24, 1997. *Mrs. Marie Quinn*, 67, of Paul Street, Hyde, attends a funeral in the morning. To those who see her, she appears to be in normal health. She telephones her son in Japan at 2 P.M., and mentions no health problems.

2: Shipman later testifies that Marie called his office at around 5:45 P.M., complaining of a weakness on her left side and asking him to visit her. This testimony was later shown to be untrue. Marie did not call his office, and at around 6:15 P.M. Shipman arrives at her house uninvited.

3: Shipman testifies that he found Marie on the floor of her kitchen, having suffered a catastrophic stroke. He claimed that she was scarcely alive when he arrived, and died within minutes. In fact, Shipman kills her with a lethal overdose of morphine. He fills out a death certificate, giving the cause of death as cardiovascular accident due to arteriosclerosis. Subsequent investigation finds the references to arteriosclerosis in Marie's medical records have been falsified.

4: Marie Quinn's body is exhumed in 13 October 1998. Toxicologists found she was killed by a morphine overdose.

years before arriving in Hyde, it appears that Shipman had been responsible for the murders of at least five people. His targeted victims belonged to a consistent demographic group. He concentrated mainly on people aged 70 years and above (although there were some younger people among his victims), often in various stages of advanced illness. Typically, during house visits Shipman would administer a lethal dose of morphine, killing the victim within minutes. He would then inform the family of their loss, his personality calm and his bearing sympathetic. He would also often attempt to steer the family down the path toward cremation as a funeral option, thereby helping to destroy all forensic evidence of his crimes.

The killing went on for years. Some local coroners and undertakers noted that the number of deaths certified by Shipman were well above the average for a general practitioner. In fact, in March 1998, by which time Shipman had been running his own office for six years, another local GP actually contacted the coroner to express concern at the suspicious number of deaths

registered by Shipman. A police investigation was started, but it would not be until the murder of Kathleen Grundy three months later that the law would truly bring down Harold Shipman.

ESCAPE THROUGH DEATH

On September 8, 1998, Shipman was charged with the murder of Kathleen Grundy. Meanwhile, forensic investigators were hard at work exhuming the bodies of many other people who had died in suspicious circumstances. Steadily, Shipman was charged with more and more murders, and by the time he went to trial on October 5, 1999, he had no fewer than 15 counts of murder against him.

During his trial, Shipman's defense team tried to present him as a devoted and widely respected local doctor, who was simply unfortunate enough to be connected with a high number of natural deaths. Yet the forensic evidence, plus explorations of his past behavior, quickly built up to a conclusive case against him. On January 31, 2000, Shipman was convicted of all 15 counts of murder and of forging Kathleen Grundy's will. He received a life sentence for each of the murders, and in July 2002 the Home Secretary David Blunkett ensured he would never be released by imposing a "whole life" tariff.

By this time, a major public enquiry had been launched into the case of Harold Shipman. It had become clear that the 15 murder convictions were just the tip of the iceberg. The inquiry was necessary both to satisfy the need to protect the public from further potential Harold Shipmans, and to satisfy the anguish of relatives who now suspected their loved ones had been unlawfully killed. It would take until 2005 before the fifth and final report into the Harold Shipman case was released, and the inquiry brought about major changes in the procedures for certifying deaths. As for Harold Shipman, at 6:20 A.M. on January 13, 2004, he was found hanging in his cell in Wakefield Prison, and pronounced dead from suicide.

◀ Under intense media and public scrutiny, Harold Shipman is taken to Preston Crown Court, in Lancashire, to face trial for murder. The arrest and trial process took more than a year to complete, and was only able to handle 15 of the known murders.

TED BUNDY

Ted Bundy remains a dark enigma in the history of serial killers. Here was someone who on the surface did not match the profile of a murderer—he was attractive, confident, well educated, courteous, and successful with women. Why, therefore, he went on to murder more than 40 women between 1974 and 1978 is a horrifying and mysterious tale.

Bundy was born Theodore Robert Cowell on November 24, 1946. His 22-year-old unmarried mother, Eleanor Louise Cowell, lived with her parents. In fact, fearing the disgrace of their daughter having a child out of wedlock, Eleanor's parents assumed the role of Theodore's mother and father—the young boy would grow up thinking that his real mother was actually his sister.

◀ July 13, 1979. Ted Bundy is here seen seated in court in Miami, Florida, charged with the killings of two Florida State University coeds. The trial led to two death sentences for Bundy.

Timeline of a Murderer— Bundy's Confirmed Victims (fatalities only)

DATE	VICTIM	AGE	DETAILS
1973			
May	Unknown	?	From Tumwater, Washington area.
1974			
February 1	Lynda Ann Healy	21	Beaten unconscious while asleep and abducted from her house.
March 12	Donna Gail Manson	19	Abducted from Evergreen State College campus, Olympia, Washington; body never recovered.
April 17	Susan Rancourt	18	Disappeared from Central Washington State College campus.
May 6	Roberta Kathleen Parks	22	Abducted from Oregon State University in Corvallis while walking to have coffee with friends.
June 1	Brenda Ball	22	Abducted from the Flame Tavern in Burien, Washington.
June 11	Georgeann Hawkins	18	Disappeared from near her sorority house, Kappa Alpha Theta, at University of Washington, Seattle.
July 14	Janice Ott	23	Abducted from Lake Sammamish State Park in Issaquah, Washington.
July 14	Denise Naslund	19	Abducted with Janice Ott—as above.
August 2	Carol Valenzuela	20	Last seen in Vancouver, Washington.
September 2	Unknown hitchhiker	17–23	Abducted from Boise, Idaho.
October 2	Nancy Wilcox	16	Last seen in Holladay, Utah.
October 18	Melissa Smith	17	Abducted from Midvale, Utah, while going to a friend's house.
October 31	Laura Aime	17	Disappeared from a Halloween party in Lehi, Utah.
November 8	Debra Kent	17	Vanished from the parking lot of a school in Bountiful, Utah.
1975			
January 12	Caryn Campbell	23	Abducted from a hotel in Aspen, Colorado.
March 15	Julie Cunningham	26	Disappeared in Vail, Colorado.
April 6	Denise Oliverson	25	Abducted while visiting her parents in Grand Junction, Colorado.
May 6	Lynette Culver	13	Abducted from a school playground at Alameda Junior High School, Pocatello, Idaho.
June 28	Susan Curtis	15	Abducted from Brigham Young University, Provo, Utah.
1978			
January 14	Lisa Levy	20	Both Lisa and Margaret were victims of the Chi Omega killings,
January 14	Margaret Bowman	21	Tallahassee, Florida. Two others survived the attack.
February 9	Kimberly Leach	12	Abducted from her junior high school in Lake City, Florida.

Ted's grandfather/father, Sam Cowell, was by all accounts a dark early influence in the young boy's life. He was an abusive and racist figure, and even by Ted's elementary school years some of his aggressive influence seemed to be rubbing off. Throughout his school life Ted expressed himself through violent tempers, and even terrorized close relatives by placing kitchen knives under their bed clothes. In 1950 Eleanor and Ted moved away from her parents to live with other relatives. She married military cook Johnnie Culpepper Bundy in 1951,

and from then on Theodore Cowell became known as Ted Bundy.

As he grew up, and survived episodes of bullying in high school, Bundy managed to cloak his true character in a seemingly approachable and confident personality. In the mid-1960s he

▼ A picture of normality—Ted Bundy helps a female friend with the dishes after a birthday party in 1975. Bundy had a charming outer persona, and was particularly confident around women.

attended the University of Washington in Seattle, and there fell deeply in love with fellow student Stephanie Brooks. Following her graduation, however, Brooks ended the relationship. Bundy was distraught, and he dropped out of college. During his educational hiatus, he also discovered a shocking truth. A visit to the birth records office in Vermont revealed his true parentage, a truly disturbing revelation that, combined with his failed romance, may well have profoundly twisted his attitude toward women.

RENAISSANCE

Bundy did not stay down for long. In 1969 he re-entered the University of Washington, and threw himself not only into his work, but also into local politics and new romances. He began to excel and his future seemed bright. In one incident he even saved a three-year-old boy from drowning, earning him praise as a hero by local police. He graduated university in 1973, and even seemed to resume his relationship with Stephanie, after they had met while Bundy was attending a Republican Party

event. (Note that he was already in a relationship with one Meg Anders at this time, who had never known that Bundy had maintained contact with his old flame during their relationship.) Neither women suspected that just a year later Bundy was about to undergo a profound transformation.

MURDER SPREE

On January 4, 1974, Bundy attempted his first murder. This was 18-year-old Joni Letz, horrifically assaulted in her Seattle apartment—her injuries

included a bed rod snapped off and forced into her vagina. Incredibly, she survived this incident. Bundy, however, was just getting started. At the beginning of February, 21-year-old Washington Law School student Lynda Ann Healy was reported missing from work (she also worked as a local weather forecaster). Police followed up on the concerns, and discovered her blood-soaked bedclothes and nightdress in her apartment, indicating that she had been brutally battered and taken from the apartment. Her remains were only discovered a year later, but police immediately opened a murder investigation.

Timeline of a Murder

1: February 9, 1978. Twelve-year-old Kimberly Leach is attending Lake City Junior High School in Lake City Florida. A few days earlier, police had checked out reports of a suspicious man in a white van, who questioned a girl about her movements while pretending to be a fire officer. The police obtain the van's license plate number, and find that the plates had earlier been stolen from a man named Randall Ragen.

2: During the school day, Kimberley leaves her purse in homeroom class, and goes back to retrieve it. She doesn't return from the short trip.

3: An eyewitness later testified that he saw a young girl being led to a white van by a man who was subsequently identified as Ted Bundy. She appeared upset.

4: The timeline of her exact murder is unclear, but it is likely that she was taken out to an area near the Suwannee River in Suwannee County, Florida. There Bundy raped her, slit her throat, and then attacked her genitals with a bladed weapon. (Later evidence showed that prior to the murder Bundy had purchased a 10in [25cm] hunting knife.)

5: April 7, 1978. Kimberly Leach's decomposing body is found in an agricultural tin shed near the Suwannee River. The body is some 40 miles (64km) to the west of her school.

◀ Bundy presented an enigmatic and unsettling figure at this final trial in 1978–79. An indication of both Bundy's confidence and intelligence came from the fact he represented himself in court.

By the time the summer of 1974 had reached its height, Bundy had murdered seven more women, some of whose bodies were never found. When other bodies began to turn up, however, police across three states—Utah, Oregon, and Washington—began to pool their information and make note of some critical similarities. The pattern of the girls' disappearances was similar, and the nature of their deaths followed the same brutal sexual manner—typically assault with a blunt instrument, followed by rape and sodomization, and eventual murder. All the victims had similar appearances—white, with their hair parted in the middle. Chillingly, the victims had a distinct resemblance to Bundy's beloved Stephanie, raising the possibility that he was re-enacting some morbid revenge fantasy for her earlier break-off of their relationship. Ironically, Bundy had actually broken off the relationship with Stephanie in February 1974.

From the reports of other girls who had briefly met Bundy, however, the police were also starting to build up a sketchy picture of the man they were looking for. Witnesses reported a handsome man driving around in a VW Beetle car, often wearing a plaster cast on his arm and leg and going by the name of "Ted." The pursuit was complicated by the fact that Bundy was now moving around. In September, he had moved to Salt Lake City, and by the following November more women began to go missing from Utah.

Yet, mercifully, Bundy made errors along the way. On November 8, 1974, his attempted abduction of one Carol DaRonch went awry—she escaped from his car and gave the police a more detailed description of both Bundy and his vehicle. (Remarkably for an intelligent man, Bundy does not seem to have changed his vehicle.) He took a break from murder, only to resume it in Colorado in early 1975, where another five women were added to his death toll.

ARREST AND ESCAPE

The life of Ted Bundy is even more morbidly remarkable on account of the fact that although he was arrested by police in 1975, and brought to trial for kidnapping, his final killings were in 1978. On August 16, 1975, a Utah Highway Patrol officer pulled over Bundy's car, his suspicions aroused by both the vehicle and its erratic driving. Following a search of the vehicle, the officer discovered rope, handcuffs, an ice pick, nylon stockings, and other suspicious items in the trunk of the car. Taking Bundy into custody, the officers then identified him as a murder suspect, based on testimony from several witnesses who had seen him in the area of the murders, or wearing the signature plaster cast. (His opening lines to his victims would often involve asking them for their assistance.) A search of his apartment unearthed equipment for making plaster casts, and other incriminating items. Finally, Bundy was charged with aggravated kidnapping.

During his trial in late February 1976, Bundy proved to be a slippery customer for the state prosecutor, providing alibis that he argued proved he couldn't have been the attacker. Yet eventually he was sentenced to 1–15 years in Utah State Penitentiary. While in prison, the police remained feverishly active on the Bundy case, hoping to link him to the numerous murders and disappearances. In October 1976, Bundy was moved to Colorado to stand trial for the murder of 23-year-old Caryn Campbell, whose body had been discovered in February 1975. With characteristic bravado, Bundy opted to conduct his own defense, and was later given access to the Pitkin County Courthouse library in Aspen for preparation. It was from there on June 7, 1977 that Bundy escaped, leaping from a second-story window.

Although he was captured eight days later, he escaped from custody again on December 30—this time he wriggled through a small aperture by unscrewing a plate around a metal ceiling-light fitting in Garfield County Jail (he had lost 30lb [14kg] in weight in preparation for the escape), and managed to make his way out through the jail's front door. He then took a flight to Florida, where he established a new life in Tallahassee. For the police back in the northeast, the trail went cold.

RAMPAGE

By this stage of his life, Bundy was an inveterate murderer, addicted to killing. A regular criminal would have laid low in his new environment, hoping to slip the police net for good. For Bundy, unfortunately, (who now called himself Chris Hagen), this was not an option. On January 14, 1978, he crept into the Chi Omega sorority house of Florida State University, where he unleashed a frenzied attack on four girls. Two of the girls were killed, while the other two escaped with serious injuries. The wounds inflicted on the dead girls included bitten-off nipples and sexual assault with a can of hairspray. Within two hours, he had also attacked another woman only six blocks away, hitting her over the head repeatedly with a length of board while masturbating with the other hand.

Bundy's final victim showed just how low his appetites could stoop. On February 9, 12-year-old Kimberley Leach was abducted, and her violated body was found in an abandoned hut two months later. Yet thankfully, the police were about to have a lucky break. On February 15, Bundy was pulled over by a police officer while driving a stolen car, and the officer arrested him after a scuffle.

The arrested man was soon identified as Bundy, and was charged with the Chi Omega murders. In a court case that gripped the nation, Bundy represented himself once again. Yet in July 1979 he

was found guilty of the two murders and sentenced to death by electric chair. A further death penalty, for the murder of Kimberley Leach, was imposed while he was on death row.

Bundy's aptitude ensured he stayed alive another 10 years, buoyed by a series of appeals. He was finally executed on January 24, 1989. Before going to the chair, he gave a prolonged televised interview with Dr. James Dobson. The interview is a chilling reminder of how psychosis and normality can sit together. Bundy finally admitted his role in a huge number of murders, talking of how an adolescent exposure to pornography fostered a desire for harder sexual imagery, then brutal sexual violence. A crowd of several hundred gathered outside the prison cheered at the pronouncement of his death.

▼ Bundy's body is taken to the Alachua County Medical Examiner's office following his execution by electric chair at 7:16 A.M. on January 24, 1989. He gave full and enlightening confession before his death.

PEDRO LOPEZ

The story of Pedro Lopez almost defies belief. Here we have an individual who was the killer of more than 300 people, almost all of them children, consigned to death at the hands of a merciless psychopath. Known in the region of his birth as the "Monster of the Andes," his nickname seems fully warranted.

Pedro Armando Lopez came into a world of rejection, cruelty, and violence. He was born in 1949 in Tolmia, Colombia, his mother being a local prostitute who would in total produce 13 children (Pedro was the seventh). Colombia at this time was a nightmare of political violence and lawlessness, and the young boy seems to have developed disturbing traits within his first years of life. At the age of eight years old his

◀ The landscape around a typical Columbian town suggests how Pedro Lopez was able to prosecute his murders so effectively. Victims could be lured from their streets into dense jungle in a matter of minutes.

mother caught him touching his sister's breasts, and threw him out on the streets to fend for himself. He was "rescued" by a local man, who then turned out to be a sickening pedophile who put Pedro through an ordeal of sexual abuse. With the terrible logic of many serial killers, however, this experience actually seemed to compel Pedro to repeat such crimes. In an interview with a journalist in 2001, Pedro stated that "I was taken in by a man who raped me over and over again. I decided then to do the same to as many young girls as possible." (*Scottish Daily Record*, February 10, 2001).

Having escaped from the clutches of his abuser, Pedro then began life on the streets, begging and stealing to survive. A momentary ray of sunshine seemed to come in the form of an American couple visiting Bogota. They spotted the disheveled boy and paid for his attendance at a local school. For reasons that are unclear, but possibly involving sexual abuse by someone in the school, Pedro soon fled and resumed his feral existence.

It was inevitable that sooner or later he would find himself in trouble with the law. At the age of 18, by which time he was principally supporting himself through car theft, he was arrested and sent to prison for seven years. Prison life continued the thread of brutality already established. He was violently gang-raped within a few days of arriving, but with an instinct for revenge he later murdered the rapists one by one, killing them with an improvised knife.

When he was finally released from prison in 1978, Pedro Lopez was a fundamentally disturbed man. He was incapable of developing proper relationships, and diverted a strong sex drive into explicit pornography and, with terrible repercussions, a burning hatred for women. Combined with his already proven capacity for violence, Lopez was about to embark on a killing spree that would make him the most prolific serial killer in history.

MONSTROUS APPETITE

Pedro Lopez's passion for killing began in earnest in 1978. He started traveling throughout Peru, Colombia, and Ecuador, targeting young girls (most of the victims were between the ages of eight and 12) from various Indian tribes, luring them away

Timeline of a Murderer—Pedro Armando Lopez

It is almost impossible to create an accurate timeline of all of Pedro Lopez's many murders. The following, therefore, provides key dates in his life up until his arrest in April 1980.

1949	Born in Tolmia, Colombia.
1957	Abandoned by mother after having been caught making sexual advances to his sister. Taken in by a man who later sexually abused him.
1963	Sexually molested at school.
1969	Arrested for car theft and sentenced to seven years in prison. Killed four inmates who had raped him.
1978	Released from prison.
1978–80	Kills an estimated 300–350 young girls in three countries.
April 1980	Arrested, convicted, and imprisoned in Ecuador.

▶ A view of Ambato, Ecuador, from the surrounding hills. At one point Lopez was killing about three Ecuadorian girls a week, later acknowledging that "I like the girls in Ecuador, they are more gentle and trusting."

Timeline of a Murder

The following timeline explains a typical Lopez murder and abduction, based upon his own testimony to journalists:

1: In a remote location in jungle or scrubland, Lopez digs a grave in preparation for the abduction and murder.

2: He patrols a busy marketplace, looking for a girl who excites his interest and who isn't watched over too closely by her parents. Her said that he looked for a girl who had "innocence and beauty."

3: Having spotted a girl, he approaches her and strikes up a conversation. Making sure her parents aren't watching, he offers the child various gifts and persuades her to come with him. He leads her out to the location of the grave he dug earlier.

4: At the site of the grave he rapes the girl, then strangles her while staring closely into her eyes. He later noted that "It took them between five and 15 minutes to die."

5: Having killed the girl, she would either be buried immediately or propped up in the grave for a horrific mock "party," in which Lopez would have a conversation with the corpse.

from busy markets with trinkets and gifts, then taking them out into isolated areas, where he had pre-dug graves, before sexually assaulting and murdering them. The rate at which he performed this ritual was terrifying, one girl going missing every few days for two years. Equally terrifying was what happened to them once they were separated from their families. He would rape them violently, gripping their throats with his hands. Then he would strangle them, always ensuring, by his own confession, that he did this by daylight so that he could see the expression in their eyes as they died. The strangulation was sometimes performed with such violence that corpses were found with their eyes dislocated. Then he would bury the small bodies in shallow graves, sometimes three or four girls occupying the same grave. In a macabre ritual following the murders, sometimes Lopez would hold "parties" for the deceased, propping them up in their graves and talking to them.

Because of the time and the remote, scattered locations of all these murders, we have few specific details of what actually occurred. We do know, however, that he came close to receiving natural justice at the hands of one Peruvian Indian tribe. Adults from the tribe caught Lopez in the act of abducting a nine-year-old girl. In response, the tribespeople opted for the ancient punishment of partly burying him, covering him with syrup and leaving him to be eaten by ants. For anyone but Lopez, such a punishment would seem utterly unjust. Yet he was saved by the intervention of an American missionary, who persuaded the Indians to release Lopez on the promise that she would hand him over to the police. She passed him over to the Peruvian authorities, who simply deported him back to Ecuador. He was free to continue murdering until 1980.

UNREPENTANT

The series of events that led up to the arrest of Pedro Lopez began in April 1980, when a flash flood near the town of Ambato in Ecuador revealed the grisly remains of four girls who had been murdered. The police began investigating the deaths, but then just a few days later a woman named Carvina Poveda had her daughter Marie grabbed by Lopez in a local marketplace. He attempted to flee with the girl in his arms, but merchants in the market came to her assistance and seized the man. They dragged him down to the police station, where initially the police officers thought they were dealing simply with a deranged drifter.

Yet Lopez now began to talk, describing how he had murdered at least 300 girls in Ecuador, Colombia, and Peru. At first the police thought him insane, but then he offered to take them to some of the places where he had buried his victims. Allowing him to do this, at one location near Ambato police were stunned to discover the bodies of 53 girls. Now they believed his story.

FREE TO KILL?

The exact details of Pedro Lopez's trial and subsequent imprisonment are vague. What is certain is that he was convicted of 110 murders in Ecuador,

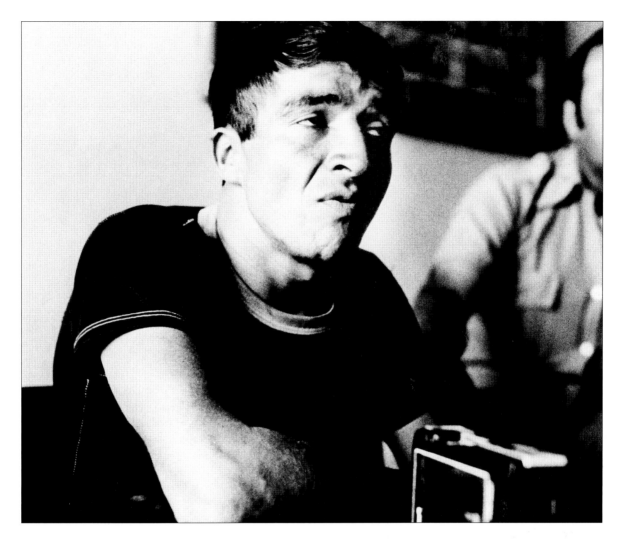

▲ Pedro Lopez's grotesque lifestyle came to light in 1980 in Ambato, Ecuador. Here he is seen confessing to police to the murder of more than 300 girls in Peru, Columbia, and Ecuador. His murder rate makes him likely to be history's most prolific serial killer.

and imprisoned. One would have thought that the scale of his crimes meant that Lopez would spend all of his remaining days in jail, but such doesn't seem to be the case. In 1998 he was released from incarceration in Ecuador, supposedly for "good behavior" and deported to Colombia, where he was rearrested and imprisoned once again. Yet according to other researchers, Lopez was confined in a psychiatric hospital in Bogotá, but was declared sane in the late 1990s and released.

If this is true, then it is possible that the world is still not safe from Pedro Lopez. In the few interviews he gave with journalists, he appeared utterly unrepentant, pinning up newspaper clippings of his exploits around the walls of his prison cell. To one journalist he noted: "It was only good if I could see her eyes, it would have been wasted in the dark I had to watch them by daylight. There is a divine moment when I have my hands around a young girl's throat. I look into her eyes and see a certain light, a spark, suddenly go out. The moment of death is enthralling and exciting. Only those who actually kill know what I mean." (*Scottish Daily Record*, February 10, 2001). It is hard to see how someone with such deep-seated instincts for murder could ever be reformed.

GARY RIDGWAY

It is a horrible testament to the casual cruelty of Gary Ridgway that he is ultimately unable to tell us how many women he strangled to death between 1982 and 2001. Although he was convicted of 48 murders, the actual number could be double that, his victims being the unfortunate and disadvantaged women of Washington State. He was dubbed the "Green River Killer," and stands as one of the worst serial killers in American history.

G ary Leon Ridgway was born on February 18, 1949 in Salt Lake City, Utah. His home life was violent and argumentative, and he did badly at school. Nevertheless, he managed to graduate from high school, and after that joined the U.S. Navy. Ridgway's time in the navy saw him sent on active service to the Vietnam War, where he experienced frequent combat while serving aboard a patrol boat in South Vietnam.

◀ King County Sheriff detectives search Gary Leon Ridgway's backyard, in Auburn, Washington, in December 2001. Improved forensic techniques were critical for securing Ridgway's 48 murder convictions.

Whether his experiences fighting in Vietnam warped his character is difficult to say; hundreds of thousands of other veterans did not return home to become serial killers. Yet once he left the military in the 1970s his personality seemed to develop two strikingly contrary threads. On the one hand he became meticulously religious, joining a local Pentecostal church and even going door to door in an attempt to convert the locals. He would never miss a service, and read his Bible on a daily basis. Yet even at the height of his apparent spirituality, far darker traits were also taking hold. He developed an abiding and deeply unhealthy interest in prostitutes, an interest that would continue through three marriages at various stages of his life. As with many serial killers who prey on prostitutes, he seemed both attracted to and repelled by women who sold sex for money. He now spotted an opportunity to indulge both sides of his attitude toward these women.

EASY PICKINGS

During the 1980s, the state of Washington was replete with prostitutes, with state and city ordinances doing little to protect vulnerable young women from descent into the trade, or help them out of it once there. Furthermore, state police were prevented from detaining or keeping records on young runaways, thereby losing the paper trail on any missing persons. In short, a killer could prey on prostitutes in the confidence that their very status would limit the effectiveness of law enforcement

Timeline of a Murderer—Gary Ridgway's Known Victims

NUMBER	VICTIM	AGE	DATE
1	Amina Agisheff	35	July 7, 1982
2	Wendy Lee Coffield	16	July 8, 1982
3	Gisele Ann Lovvorn	17	July 17, 1982
4	Debra Lynn Bonner	23	July 25, 1982
5	Marcia Fay Chapman	31	August 1, 1982
6	Cynthia Jean Hinds	17	August 11, 1982
7	Opal Charmaine Mills	16	August 12, 1982
8	Terry Rene Milligan	16	August 29, 1982
9	Mary Bridget Meehan	18	September 15, 1982
10	Debra Lorraine Estes	15	September 20, 1982
11	Linda Jane Rule	16	September 26, 1982
12	Denise Darcel Bush	23	October 8, 1982
13	Shawnda Leea Summers	16	October 9, 1982
14	Shirley Marie Sherrill	18	October 20–22, 1982
15	Colleen Renee Brockman	15	December 24, 1982
16	Alma Ann Smith	18	March 3, 1983
17	Delores LaVerne Williams	17	March 8–14, 1983
18	Gail Lynn Mathews	23	April 10, 1983
19	Andrea M. Childers	19	April 14, 1983
20	Sandra Kay Gabbert	17	April 17, 1983
21	Kimi-Kai Pitsor	16	April 17, 1983
22	Marie M. Malvar	18	April 30, 1983
23	Carol Ann Christensen	21	May 3, 1983
24	Angela Marie Girdner	16	May 1983
25	Martina Theresa Authorlee	18	May 22, 1983

investigations. Ridgway himself later admitted that this was the overriding reason why he focused his murderous activities on prostitutes: "I picked prostitutes as my victims because I hate most prostitutes and I did not want to pay them for sex. I also picked prostitutes as victims because they were easy to pick up without being noticed. I knew they would not be reported missing right away and might never be reported missing. I picked prostitutes because I thought I could kill as many of them as I wanted without getting caught."

He would begin testing out his theory in July 1982. On July 15, schoolchildren discovered the body of 16-year-old prostitute Wendy Lee Coffield in the Green River running through Kent County, stripped naked and dead from strangulation. A month later the Green River gave up the body of Deborah Bonner, again strangled, and two days later two more bodies appeared—31-year-old Marcia Chapman and 17-year-old Cynthia Hinds. A police search of the area produced another body, that of a 16-year-old girl. Sharing both vocation and the manner of their death, the bodies led police to the unavoidable conclusion that they had a serial killer operating in their locality.

EVASION

The great tragedy of the case of Gary Ridgway was that he continued to kill women frequently despite the formation of substantial police task forces in response. Two major task forces were formed in 1980–3, and they began regular patrols of the

NUMBER	VICTIM	AGE	DATE
26	Cheryl Lee Wims	18	May 23, 1983
27	Yvonne "Shelly" Antosh	19	May 31, 1983
28	Carrie Ann Rois	15	May 31–June 13, 1983
29	Constance Elizabeth Naon	19	June 8, 1983
30	Kelly Marie Ware	22	July 18, 1983
31	Tina Marie Thompson	21	July 25, 1983
32	April Dawn Buttram	16	August 18, 1983
33	Debbie May Abernathy	26	September 5, 1983
34	Tracy Ann Winston	19	September 12, 1983
35	Maureen Sue Feeney	19	September 28, 1983
36	Mary Sue Bello	25	October 11, 1983
37	Pammy Annette Avent	15	October 26, 1983
38	Delise Louise Plager	22	October 30, 1983
39	Kimberly L. Nelson	21	November 1, 1983
40	Lisa Yates	19	December 23, 1983
41	Mary Exzetta West	16	February 6, 1984
42	Cindy Anne Smith	17	March 21, 1984
43	Patricia Michelle Barczak	19	October 17, 1986
44	Roberta Joseph Hayes	21	After February 7, 1987
45	Marta Reeves	36	March 5, 1990
46	Patricia Yellowrobe	38	January 1998
47	Unidentified White Female	12–17	Died prior to May 1983
48	Unidentified Black Female	18–27	1982–1984
49	Unidentified White Female	14–18	December 14–18 ,1980

Timeline of a Murder

1: It is the evening of April 30, 1983. Marie Malvar is standing on the corner of 216th Street and Pacific Highway South in King County, Seattle. Her boyfriend and pimp, Bobby Woods, sat in a nearby car.

2: Gary Ridgway pulls up to the street corner and propositions Marie, who then gets into his pickup and drives away. Bobby Woods sets out to follow the pickup, but loses it at a red traffic light.

3: Ridgway takes Marie back to his house on Military Road. There he strangles her in the bedroom, and later

that night dumps her body in nearby woodland.

4: When Marie does not come home for the night, Bobby Woods and Marie's father, Jose, drive around the nearby area, trying to spot the pickup. They eventually see the vehicle after about half an hour's driving; it is parked in Ridgway's drive. They pass the details to Des Moines police, although the information does not lead to an arrest.

5: Marie's body lays undiscovered until September 2003, when it is found more than 20 years after the murder occurred.

Green River area by both uniformed and undercover officers. The media, however, was also in an excited state over the murders, and on occasions the positions of stakeout officers were actually revealed by hovering television news helicopters.

Yet as bodies mounted up on a regular basis, the police came no closer to catching the killer. Some time was wasted investigating an ex-offender named Melvin Wayne Foster, who fitted an FBI psychological profile developed for the police, and who was pulled in and failed a lie detector test. He was finally eliminated from the investigation, however, when killings continued even as Foster was kept under heavy police surveillance.

By the end of 1983, the police had discovered the bodies of a dozen young women. In actuality, by this stage Ridgway had killed at least 40 women, the vast majority of them between the ages of 16 and 25. The murders had a repetitive pattern to them. Ridgway himself later told investigators: "I killed some of them outside. I remember leaving each woman's body in the place where she was found … I killed most of them in my house near Military Road, and I killed a lot of them in my truck not far from where I picked them up." His preferred method of killing was always strangulation, either using his powerful arms or some form of ligature, such as a piece of wire or an item of the girl's clothing.

He occasionally seemed to play mind games with the police. On May 3, 1983, for example, he murdered 21-year-old Carole Ann Christensen with a piece of fishing line, then draped her body with

two trout fish and a wine bottle, with a pile of sausage meat next to her body and a bag pulled over her head. The purpose of this scene is unclear, but Ridgway worked in the full knowledge that his murder victims would be found, and was possibly attempting to create some sort of psychological puzzle, real or mocking, for the investigators.

At several points the police did come tantalizingly close to apprehending Ridgway. In April 1983, 18-year-old Marie Malvar got into his pickup truck. What Ridgway didn't know was that he was being followed by her boyfriend and pimp, Bobby Woods. Woods eventually lost sight of the pickup in the city traffic, but when Marie did not come home that night he drove around until he spotted the vehicle parked outside Ridgway's home. He reported the sighting to the Des Moines police, but it was not until November 1983 that the information resulted in Ridgway being pulled in for interview by the King County police. Ridgway denied everything convincingly. In fact, Ridgway became a major suspect from his known associations with at least three of the victims, but on two occasions he passed a polygraph test, so was passed over.

NEW INVESTIGATION

Ridgway seems to have done most of his killing between 1982 and 1987. Following a murder around February 7, 1987, his rate dropped significantly—there were "only" two known murders between 1990 and 2001, although there are likely to have been more. Certainly, police efforts to investigate the murders had weakened during the late

1980s, but then pressure from relatives of the victims stirred up the cold cases.

In 2001, the new King County sheriff, Dave Reichert, reinvigorated investigations by using the far more sophisticated forensic and DNA techniques that were now available. Going back to the forensic samples from the earliest murders, the police were able to extract DNA from semen found on the bodies. On September 10, 2001, the DNA sample made a positive match with samples taken from Ridgway in April 1987.

Ridgway was arrested on November 30, 2001. Despite early protestations of his innocence, the forensic evidence mounted up so conclusively that he decided to enter a plea bargain in an attempt to avoid the death penalty. Negotiating with such a hideous individual was unpalatable, but it provided the best opportunity to find out exactly what happened to so many of his victims, and to recover more bodies. In November 2003, Ridgway confessed to 48 charges of first-degree murder, a confession that led to his receiving 48 life sentences the following December, plus an additional 10 years for evidence tampering relating to each of his 48 confessed victims.

Having been sentenced to spend the rest of his natural life in prison, Ridgway subsequently modified some of his confessions to indicate that he had killed many more women. (A total of 49 victims have been confirmed.) In an interview he confessed to having killed 65 women, and in another he spoke of murdering 71 women. In truth, he had killed so many that he couldn't entirely remember the final horrible tally.

▼ **King County Deputy Prosecutor Jeff Baird speaks during Ridgway's sentencing. Ridgway's assistance in finding bodies saved him from the death penalty.**

H. H. HOLMES

Many would class the individuals in this book as evil. Yet H. H. Holmes seems to belong in a class of his own. There is no firm evidence as to how many people he murdered during the late nineteenth century, but it probably exceeds 50. However, it is not so much the death toll but the manner and ruthless intelligence of the murders that still carry the power to shock.

Later in life, as he waited for the final confirmation of his death sentence, H. H. Holmes wrote various confused accounts of his life. At times he presented himself as the victim of a simple miscarriage of justice, yet in other passages his confessions seemed to reach much closer to the mark: "I was born with the devil in me. I was born with the Evil One standing as my sponsor beside the bed where I was ushered into

◄ "The Castle" in Chicago was a three-story hotel created to H. H. Holmes' personal design in the early 1890s. The final number of victims who were murdered there is still unknown.

this world. He has been with me ever since." By the time he reached the end of his life on May 7, 1896, twitching for 15 minutes on the end of the rope following a botched hanging, few would question this judgment.

The name H. H. Holmes was assumed much later in life, as part of a fabricated respectable persona. He was actually born Herman Webster Mudgett on May 16, 1861 in Gilmanton, New Hampshire. Herman was known for being a bright but rather odd young man, for beneath the surface some morbid tendencies were stirring. His home life was not a happy one, trapped between a bullying father, Levi Horton Mudgett, and a diffident mother, Theodate. He was also bullied at school, his rather frail and academic appearance making him an easy target. Herman's only friend, a boy called Tom, died in front of his eyes after falling from the landing of a deserted house into which they had crept. And in what proved to be a formative incident, on one occasion two bullies dragged him into the office of the village doctor, and forced him into the arms of a medical skeleton, deeply traumatizing the boy.

It was from around his early teens that Herman began to show something of an unhealthy interest in dissection and death. He began experimenting on animals, masking the mutilation of everything from rabbits to dogs under the pretense of medical examination. He nonetheless kept his academic momentum going and as a young adult eventually graduated with a medical degree from the University of Michigan at Ann Arbor in 1884. His time at university, however, was also a period in which he developed the sinister business acumen that would support him throughout his life. He would take out life insurance policies on corpses stolen from the medical school laboratory, mutilate them as if they had been involved in accidents, and then claim the insurance policy on the body. By this time he was also married—he wed Clara A. Lovering of Alton, New Hampshire, in 1878. Later in life he would marry two more women, Myrta Z. Belknap in 1887 and Georgiana Yoke in 1894, both without obtaining divorces. And, as well as being a bigamist, he was a serial philanderer, women being easily attracted by his charming, successful, and attractive character. Yet so many of those who fell under his personal magnetism would end up dying at his hands.

THE CASTLE

In 1886, Herman moved to Chicago, by this time having assumed the name of Dr. H. H. Holmes. He began working as a drugstore assistant. The drugstore's owner, E. S. Holton, was dying of cancer, and his wife looked after the store with a new assistant. Through his powers of persuasion,

Timeline of a Murderer—Known Victims of H. H. Holmes

Here are just a few of Holmes' murders, although the actual death toll is likely to exceed 50.

December 1892	Emeline Cigrand; suffocated after having been locked in an airtight room; Holmes turned her body into a medical skeleton.
c. July 1893	Nannie Williams and Minnie Williams; Holmes murdered both sisters, after striking up a romance with Minnie.
September 1894	Benjamin Pitezel; Holmes' partner in an insurance fraud; burned to death to give the appearance of a laboratory accident.
October 1894	Howard Pitezel (8); drugged and strangled, and his body cut up and incinerated in a stove.
October/ November 1894	Nellie (11) and Alice Pitezel (15); the two girls were locked in a specially adapted trunk and gassed to death.

▲ Two photos of Dr. Henry Howard Holmes, born Herman Webster Mudgett in 1861. Like many serial killers, Holmes presented an attractive outward manner, and had no shortage of female admirers.

Holmes managed to purchase the drugstore from the emotionally fragile owners, although they remained living above the premises. When E. S. Holton died, Holmes simply murdered Mrs. Holton, telling anyone asking after her that she had gone to live with relatives in California. Soon the drugstore was turning over a tidy profit in his name, and combined with income from other questionable sources, he was ready to put in place his master plan.

It was known as the "Castle." This three-story hotel, constructed on a vacant lot opposite Holmes' drugstore, was created according to Holmes' personal design. It was an almost Escher-like labyrinth, with features such as blind corridors, hallways set at bizarre angles, concealed chambers and shafts, secret passageways, staircases that led to nothing but brick walls, and soundproofed chambers with peepholes fitted into the doors. Gas pipes were diverted into several bedrooms and chambers, through which Holmes could divert lethal gases at the moment of his choosing, all from the comfort of his own office. In the basement, Holmes created his very own torture chamber and dissection suite, which included pits of lime and acid, and cremation furnaces. In short, Holmes had created the ultimate house of horror, a place of chaos, disorientation, and death in which he could indulge his sickest visions. The only reason that the building contractors did not suspect his intentions was that he kept firing them after only a few weeks on the job, ensuring that nobody could put together the puzzle that was the Castle.

KILLING HOUSE

As the Castle was completed in 1891–93, timed to take guests for Chicago's World Fair that year,

Timeline of a Murder—1890–91

1: 1890. *Ned Connor* arrives in Chicago to work for Holmes as a watchmaker and jeweler. Connor brought with him his attractive wife, Julia, and their daughter Pearl, and they move into the apartment above Holmes' store.

2: Holmes quickly becomes obsessed with the red-haired, green-eyed Julia, and hires her as his bookkeeper while also trying to seduce her. She eventually gives in to his advances, and Ned moves away, having lost his family.

3: With Ned gone, Holmes takes out several large insurance policies on Julia and Pearl, naming himself beneficiary. By now (1891), Holmes is living in the Castle.

4: 1891. Holmes strikes up a new relationship with a woman named *Minnie Williams*. Julia is angered by this turn of events, especially as she is by this point carrying Holmes' child. Holmes insists that he perform an abortion.

5: Julia is led down into the basement of the Castle. There Holmes both aborts his child and murders Julia. He disposes of her body in one of his stoves. Shortly afterward he kills Pearl with chloroform—her bones were later found stuffed into a hole in the middle of the basement floor.

Holmes began a simply breathtaking reign of terror. Dozens of staff and guests went missing (he kept a high turnover of both to avoid suspicion), most of the victims being females to whom Holmes was attracted. They died in a variety of vile ways—suffocated in airtight or gas-filled rooms; tortured on a stretching rack down in the basement; dissected with surgical instruments while still alive; burned to death (some of his rooms were fireproof, so he could fill them with gas then ignite the vapors). He even made money out of the whole ghastly business. He would often strip the bodies of all their flesh and then sell the skeletons to medical institutions. Those bodies that he kept he destroyed in vats of acid or in his crematoriums.

It is hard to know just how many people were murdered in the Castle. Although there are a verified 27 murders committed by Holmes, the actual number could well over 50, based upon people who disappeared when in contact with this monstrous man. Yet in 1894, the weight of the law finally caught up with H. H. Holmes.

REVEALED

It is incredible to think that so many people could disappear without the finger of suspicion pointing at Holmes. What finally led to his undoing, however, was an insurance fraud. Benjamin Pitezel, one of Holmes' employees, partnered up with Holmes for a scam. In 1893 Pitezel took out a $10,000 life insurance policy on himself, on the agreement that Holmes would find and disfigure a dead body, claim that it was Pitezel's, and the two

men could share the money between them. In the event, Holmes simply murdered Pitezel by literally burning him alive (to corroborate the story of a laboratory accident) and took off with three of Pitezel's children, while stringing Mrs Pitezel (who had her two remaining children) along with various stories. Holmes traveled through the northern United States and Canada, and on the way murdered all three children—he killed the young boy, cut him up into small pieces and burned them on a stove, and gassed the remaining two young girls to death in a small trunk.

Shortly before this tragic sequence of events, in July 1894 Holmes was briefly imprisoned for his involvement in a horseracing scam. During his time in prison, Holmes indiscreetly confessed to a cellmate, Marion Hedgepeth, about his intended life insurance scam, and offered to pay Hedgepeth $500 if he could find him a "trusted" lawyer would assist him with any legal difficulties. Hedgepeth was good to his word, but Holmes did not honor the agreed payment—Hedgepeth subsequently told the police about the Pitezel scam, and the Pinkerton National Detective Agency sent out agents to hunt down Holmes for fraud, and potentially murder.

Holmes was eventually arrested on November 17, 1894 in Boston, good detective work having discovered the bodies of the Pitezel children. The police now conducted a thorough search of the Castle. What they found there shocked even the most hardened homicide officers. The basement in particular was full of human remains, and evidence of killing lay in other rooms, corridors, and passageways. It was clear that Holmes was a monstrous personality. He was convicted for the murder of Benjamin Pitezel, and having been sentenced to death he subsequently confessed to 27 other murders. He was hanged on May 7, 1896 at Philadelphia County Prison, his execution cutting short the opportunities for more confessions. In an ironic last request, Holmes asked that his body be buried in concrete so that he would not be dug up and dissected, just as he had cut up so many of his victims. This being agreed, he went to the gallows in an apparently calm and contented frame of mind, showing no signs of regret for the carnage he left behind him.

▼ The World's Columbian Exposition in 1893 attracted thousand of visitors to Chicago, some of whom fatally stayed in Holmes' hotel.

ALBERT FISH

The case of Albert Fish both defies belief and tests the strongest of stomachs. He was one of the most grotesque child murderers in U.S. history, although it is unclear how many victims fell to his methods of torture, mutilation, and cannibalism. It seems plausible that only a man who had passed fully into insanity could be capable of such crimes, although the legal system of the day disagreed with such a diagnosis.

A lbert Fish's life reads like a case study in psychosis. He was born Hamilton Fish on May 19, 1870 in Washington, DC, and life immediately went wrong for the boy. His father, one of several members of the family with a known history of mental illness, died of a heart attack when he was just one year old, and by the time he was five he had been placed in an orphanage. He remained there for the next four

◄ Police pump water from the well in the grounds of the house where Albert Fish killed Grace Budd, December 16, 1934. Bones were discovered at the site that confirmed the grisly murder.

▲ Albert Fish is led into homicide court by detective William King. Had it not been for King's intelligence and persistence during a six-year search, more children might have fallen victim to Fish's appetites.

Timeline of a Murderer—Known Victims of Albert Fish

DATE	VICTIM	AGE	DETAILS
July 15, 1924	Francis X. McDonnell	8	Strangled to death on Long Island.
February 11, 1927	William Gaffney	4	Kidnapped, tortured, and then extensively cannibalized.
June 3, 1928	Grace Budd	10	Taken away from her home before being strangled and cannibalized; Fish sent a letter describing the murder to Mrs. Budd in 1934.
February 15, 1932	Mary Ellen O'Connor	16	Abducted and murdered in Far Rockaway, New York; her mutilated body was discovered near to a house Fish had been painting.

years, during which time a strange tendency emerged. Fish was whipped and beaten by orphanage staff, often as part of a communal punishment, but he actually appeared to enjoy the experience, even developing an erection while being struck.

When he was nine years old, Fish returned to the custody of his mother, who had managed to find employment enough to support her son. The return, however, he did not bring mental stability. A homosexual experience at the age of 12 developed into experimentation with coprophagia and drinking urine, and by the time he reached his early twenties he was intermittently working as a male prostitute and also frequenting male brothels. Perhaps sensing his moral compass was going somewhat astray, his mother arranged a marriage for him in 1898, and he went on to have six children. Luckily for the children, he does not appear to have violently abused them, although they certainly witnessed some odd and deviant behavior. For example, when there was a full moon their father would ingest large quantities of red meat and then howl at the sky. Unsurprisingly, his wife left him in 1917 for another man, although the children remained in Fish's custody.

Fish's long-term affection for pain now began to express itself in terrifying sadomasochistic activities, which included pushing needles into his genitals and pelvic area. At the time of his final arrest in 1934, he was found to have at least 21 needles stuck into his pelvis and perineum. Other self-punishing activities included smacking himself with a nail-studded bat. Adding to this picture of insanity was his tendency to send large numbers of obscene letters to various women, whose names he gleaned from classified advertisements or other public sources.

FRENZIED KILLINGS

Much of what we know of Fish's violent and murderous activities is vague and unsubstantiated, although the murders that we do know of give credence to his later confession statements. He became a house painter in 1898, and thereby traveled widely in his work. Around this time he began to torture, sexually assault, and kill children, taking the lives of dozens of young victims, according to his own estimates. One of the key problems of forming an actual list of victims is that he deliberately targeted children from poor neighborhoods (particularly African-Americans), and also the mentally handicapped, relying on the fact that police disinterest in such sectors of society would lead to lacklustre investigations. We do know of two of Fish's attacks in the early twentieth century, one on a young boy in Wilmington, Delaware, in 1910, and the stabbing of a mentally handicapped African-American child in 1919. Then on July 15, 1924, eight-year-old Francis X. McDonnell went missing from outside his home in Charlton Woods, Staten Island. A strange, disheveled old man had been seen in the area shortly before. A police search later found the boy's body in the woods, horribly beaten, naked, and strangled with his own suspenders.

This was Fish's work, yet he was capable of sinking to even viler depths. On February 11, 1927, Fish kidnapped four-year-old William Gaffney, and gave full expression to the most hideous corners of his personality. A later written confession of the crime, given to Gaffney's mother from Sing Sing prison following his arrest in 1934, made grotesque and harrowing reading, and showed the monstrosity Fish had become. In excrutiating detail, Fish explained to the naturally distraught mother how he had stripped William, tied him up and then beaten him with a heavy, home-made cat-o'-nine-tails. He then killed the boy and took home parts of his body to eat, even explaining the cooking techniques he used to make a hideous stew.

According to Fish, many other children met a fate just as appalling as that of poor William Gaffney. Yet it would be many years before Fish was finally taken off the streets, even though he was incarcerated on several occasions before 1934 for petty crimes and also for psychiatric evaluation, following arrests on account of his habit of writing obscene letters. Indeed, it would be a letter that led to his final arrest.

GRACE BUDD

In 1928, Fish kidnapped 10-year-old Grace Budd from her family in New York. He had visited the family under the name Frank Howard, under the pretence of hiring 18-year-old Edward Budd, Grace's brother, for laboring work. (Edward had placed a classified ad offering himself for employment.) On his second visit to the house, he convinced Grace's parents to let him take their daughter to a birthday party. They consented, and let Fish lead off their young daughter to a truly appalling death (see "Timeline of a Murder").

The disappearance of a girl from a middle-class neighborhood now sparked a greater response from the police. The search and investigation led down several blind paths, including the arrest of one Charles Edward Pope in September 1930, although he was found innocent at his trial. The lead investigator on the Budd case, William F. King, was a tenacious character, however, and kept chipping away at the case over the course of six years. In November 1934 came an unexpected development. A letter arrived at the Budd household, addressed to Mrs. Budd. In utterly horrifying detail, the author of the letter described to Mrs. Budd how he had murdered, mutilated, and eaten her daughter.

The letter also attempted to explain the origins of his appetites. It began as follows (grammatical and spelling errors in the original text are preserved here):

Timeline of a Murder

1: June 3, 1928. Albert Fish, masquerading as "Frank Howard," a farmer from Farmingdale, New York, visits for the second time the Budd family at 406 West 15th Street, New York, under the pretence of hiring 18-year-old Edward Budd for employment.

2: He convinces the parents of the household, Delia and Albert Budd, to let him take their 10-year-old daughter, *Grace*, to an evening birthday party held at his sister's house. During his time at their home, they have lunch together and Grace sits on his lap. He later said that at that moment "I made up my mind to eat her."

3: Delia and Albert Budd consent to Fish's offer. He leads Grace away, taking a train to the Bronx then Worthington, Westchester. In Worthington, he takes Grace to an empty house. On their arrival, he tells her to stay outside while he goes inside. She remains out in the garden, picking wild flowers. Fish, meanwhile, goes upstairs and takes off all his clothes.

4: Fish calls Grace from the top bedroom window, telling her to come inside. As she is coming upstairs, Fish hides in a closet. Once she enters the room, he leaps from the closet and grabs her. The young girl begins to cry.

5: Grace begins to fight back, kicking and biting. He nevertheless strips her naked and then chokes her to death. In his later letter to Mrs. Budd, he made a point of saying that he did not rape her, and that she died, in his words, "a virgin."

6: Once the girl is dead, Fish cuts her body into small pieces and retains the flesh. Over a period of nine days, he cooks and eats almost her entire body.

"My dear Mrs. Budd,

"In 1894 a friend of mine shipped as a deck hand on the Steamer Tacoma, Capt. John Davis. They sailed from San Francisco for Hong Kong China. On arriving there he and two others went ashore and got drunk. When they returned the boat was gone.

"At that time there was famine in China. Meat of any kind was from $1 to 3 Dollars a pound. So great was the suffering among the very poor that all children under 12 were sold for food in order to keep others from starving. A boy or girl under 14 was not safe in the street. You could go in any shop and ask for steak—chops—or stew meat. Part of the naked body of a boy or girl would be brought out and just what you wanted cut from it. A boy or girls behind which is the sweetest part of the body and sold as veal cutlet brought the highest price.

"John staid there so long he acquired a taste for human flesh. On his return to N.Y. he stole two boys one 7 one 11. Took them to his home stripped them naked tied them in a closet. Then burned everything they had on. Several times every day and night he spanked them— tortured them—to make their meat good and tender.

"First he killed the 11 year old boy, because he had the fattest ass and of course the most meat on it. Every part of his body was Cooked and eaten except the head—bones and guts. He was Roasted in the oven (all of his ass), boiled, broiled, fried and stewed. The little boy was next, went the

▶ The unfortunate Grace Budd, murdered by Fish on June 3, 1928. Fish later stated that he set his mind on eating her within minutes of their meeting.

same way. At that time, I was living at 409 E 100 st., near—right side. He told me so often how good Human flesh was I made up my mind to taste it."

Coming so long after the murder, and without the forensic technology available today, the letter could have been a dead end. But then King noticed the letters "NYPCBA" stamped on the paper, and discovered that they stood for New York Private Chauffeurs' Benevolent Association. He contacted the organization, and a janitor who worked there told him that he had taken some of the stationery to his lodgings at 200 East 52nd Street, but left it there when he moved to another address. The landlady of

the lodgings described how a man, fitting the description of "Frank Howard" but called Albert Fish, had stayed there, and in fact still returned periodically to pick up checks sent to him by his son. Now all King had to do was wait.

On December 13, 1934, Detective King received a phone call telling him that Albert Fish was around at the rooming house. By the time King arrived, the scruffy looking old man was sitting down having a cup of tea. The detective simply asked whether he was Albert Fish, to which Fish responded by attacking him with a razor blade. King easily overpowered Fish in the struggle, and took him into custody.

FINAL VERDICT

Once arrested and behind bars, Fish now rather gleefully divulged the details of his crimes, describing numerous child murders committed over the last three decades. Grace Budd's much-diminished remains were subsequently discovered on the basis of this evidence. He also became the focus of intense interest from psychiatrists, who were fascinated and appalled by the man's

psychosis, especially once an X-ray had revealed the needles stuck inside his own body.

In his trial for the murder of Grace Budd in 1935 he pleaded insanity, claiming that he heard the voice of God telling him to kill children. Although there seemed to be a compelling case for arguing insanity, Fish was found both sane and guilty by the jury, and sentenced to death by electric chair. Having been sentenced, he then confessed to or was linked with several more murders, providing harrowing details in some instances, such as in the case of William Gaffney.

Albert Fish went to the electric chair at 11:06 P.M. on January 16, 1936 in Sing Sing prison. The prospect of violent death held no terrors for him. He actually made his final journey in a state of high excitement, professing that electrocution would be "the supreme thrill of my life."

▼ Police officers halt traffic to permit the jury at the Albert Fish trial to return to court after lunch. The jury had to sit through complex psychiatric evidence, plus harrowing details of Fish's crimes, but ultimately found Fish both sane and guilty.

JOACHIM KROLL

No one knows how many people Joachim Kroll murdered in his lifetime. He was certainly responsible for 13 murders, to which he confessed, but those could be the tip of the iceberg. What is certain, however, was that the nature of the murders he committed indicate a deep-seated perversion, and an uncontrollable lust for death and mutilation.

The life of Joachim Kroll has a certain resonance with that of Andrei Chikatilo, at least in the early developmental years. Kroll was born on April 17, 1933 in Hindenburg, Upper Silesia, a part of Germany on the German–Polish border. Germany went to war in 1939, but the war came to the Kroll family in person in 1944 and 1945, when the Soviets advanced into German territory from the east.

◀ The Ruhr area of Germany gave Kroll a large population base among which he could hunt. He tended to pick up his victims at train or bus stations, and take them to more isolated locations.

Timeline of a Murder

1: February 8, 1955. Joachim Kroll is walking along a rural road near the town of Lüdinghausen, Germany, when he encounters 19-year-old *Irmgard Strehl*. She is wearing a green coat, and carries a book bag with study materials inside.

2: Kroll strikes up a conversation with the young woman, and makes a promise that he will give her something if she walks with him into the woods. The girl complies.

3: Once in the woods, Kroll attempts to embrace and kiss Irmgard. She resists, and Kroll loses all control. He drags her into a nearby barn, and stabs her in the neck (he carries a folding lock-knife).

4: Kroll then strangles Irmgard to ensure that she is dead, before he rapes the body. At some point during the attack, probably after the rape, he disembowels her with his knife.

5: Depending on the sources, Kroll either leaves the body where it lies or disposes of it in nearby bushes.

These were times in which the Russian forces revisited terrible cruelties on the German population, and the Krolls did not escape. They suffered from periods of acute hunger, and Joachim's father was taken prisoner by the Russians, thereafter being deported to the Soviet Union. He never returned, having been probably worked to death as slave labor.

Throughout all this upheaval, it is unsurprising that the young Joachim developed poorly. His educational performance was substandard compared to other children around him, so much so that he was nearly classified as mentally retarded. The immediate postwar years for Joachim brought continued hardship, living with his mother and six other siblings in a house in the industrialized Ruhr area of West Germany, to which the family had fled at the end of the war.

In January 1955, the cement holding the family, and Joachim, together disintegrated when his mother died. By this time he was 22 years old, and the complexities of the psychology would express themselves in extreme violence within a matter of weeks of his mother's passing.

SERIAL APPETITES

On February 8, 1955, Joachim Kroll stabbed, raped, disemboweled, and strangled 19-year-old Irmgard Strehl. The attack was utterly frenzied, and a postmortem later revealed that the rape had occurred after the unfortunate girl had been killed. It is hard even to conceive how Kroll could push his depravity lower than this incident, but over the next two decades of murder he would plumb new depths. He killed again within a year, this time abducting, raping, and strangling 12-year-old Erika Schuleter in the town of Kirchellen. In 1959, we know of two additional murders. The first one occurred on June 16, the victim being Klara Frieda Tesmer, 24, who was killed in the Rheinhausen district of Duisburg. In a horrible twist, another man was actually arrested for the murder, and he later hanged himself in despair. The next victim was 16-year-old Manuela Knodt, killed on July 26 in the city park in Essen. In a sadistic new twist to Kroll's modus operandi, on this occasion he actually sliced sections of flesh from her buttocks and thighs, and took them home with him to eat. Cannibalism would become one of the "signatures" of Kroll's reign as a serial killer. His preference was for the internal organs, but he would also take hands and other external parts.

Kroll gradually established a method to his murders. He generally took a bus or train to an isolated station, then walked around until he spotted a potential victim. He would then follow her until she was away from others, before pouncing and dragging her into fields or wasteland, where she was killed. He also left police with much evidence that today would be forensically invaluable, including copious semen samples. (He would sometimes masturbate prolifically over the corpse, so much so that on occasions the police believe that they were dealing with a gang attack.) Kroll himself, with the benefit of hindsight, also presented something of an odd personality. He seemed to have an excessive fondness for children, particularly little girls, and in his apartment he had a large collection of dolls, which he used to treat as companions. This companionship, however, extended to acts of strangulation on inflatable sex dolls, a practice no doubt hidden from the world outside, which generally regarded him as an avuncular and unthreatening character.

Following the killing of Manuela Knodt, the police once again arrested the wrong man. Even so, it appears that at this point Kroll took something of a break from his killing spree. When he did resume his activities, in early 1962, he did so with increased tempo. His first victim of this new phase was 12-year-old Barbara Bruder, who disappeared from the town of Burscheid and was never seen again. (Kroll later confessed to her murder, but her body was never found.) Next came 13-year-old Petra Giese, then Monika Tafel, also 13. The last two victims also had body parts removed for later cannibalism. With three victims in such a short space of time, and genuine fear among local parents, there was much pressure upon the police to find their man and make an arrest. Unfortunately, once again their investigation led them in the wrong direction—a 34-year-old pedophile was taken into custody and charged, and he hanged himself.

THE ROAD TO ARREST

To be fair to the police investigating the "Ruhr hunter," as the killer was nicknamed, Kroll seems to have had an unusual degree of patience, and a certain control over his appetites. For he now again waited another three years before committing his next murder, the break seriously disrupting the continuity of any homicide investigation. When he did kill again, the murder was of a rather different kind. On August 22, 1965, he attacked a young courting couple in a car parked in an isolated spot in Duisburg-Großenbaumand. Kroll first forced the man, Hermann Schimtz, out of the car before stabbing him several times, with fatal results. He probably committed this murder so that he could focus his attentions upon the young girl, but she reacted with presence of mind, speeding off in the

▲ Although Kroll here appears slightly unnerving, it remains hard to match the crimes with his appearance. Children and young people tended to trust him on first meeting, often with fatal results.

car despite the fact that Kroll had slashed one of the tires.

The girl's survival provided the police with one of the first visual descriptions of the Ruhr hunter, but it would still be several years before he fell into their hands. In that time, he continued killing and the list of people wrongfully accused grew. After the death of Ursula Rohling in September 1966 (killed by Kroll in parkland north of Duisburg), the police focused their attentions on Adolf Schickel, Ursula's boyfriend. In despair at the accusation, Adolf hanged himself, just like many of his predecessors.

Kroll would go on killing until 1976. The age range of his victims began to vary wildly. On

July 12, 1969, for example, he crept into the home of Maria Hettgen, 61, who lived in the town of Hückeswagen, near Cologne. There he raped and strangled the elderly woman. Yet the undeniable tendency of Kroll's victim selection was toward youth. He killed several children of single digits age, and on July 3, 1976 he slaughtered his youngest victim, four-year-old Marion Ketter. The poor child disappeared from a playground in Duisburg, and the police began a frantic search of the area, going house to house in their investigations.

Now, however, came the lucky break (lucky for the police, that is). A resident in Kroll's apartment block confronted him over a blocked toilet. In either a complacent or confessional reply, Kroll said that the toilet was "full of guts." Sure enough, when the neighbor went to look, the toilet was full with bloody pieces of flesh, although he did not

▼ The surveillance room at Rheinbach prison, where Kroll was held following his conviction for murder. He died there of a heart attack on July 1, 1991, having served only nine years of his imprisonment.

know whether the remains were human or animal. Knowing of the disappearance of Marion Ketter, the neighbor contacted the local police, who came round to the apartment with a plumber, who cleaned out the system. In the process, they found numerous internal organs, of the right size to belong to a child. Deeply unnerved by their discovery, the police officers confronted Kroll about their findings. He assured them that the remains were from a rabbit he had skinned and gutted earlier, but it was clear to the officers that the organs were much too large for a rabbit. They gained access to Kroll's apartment. In the kitchen, bubbling away on stove, was a pot of stew. Curiously stirring the stew, an officer found that one of the ingredients was a tiny human hand. Further searches revealed grotesque bags of human meat in the refrigerator and freezer. Kroll was immediately arrested.

The Kroll arrest has a similarity to that of Dennis Nilsen, and like Nilsen, Kroll quickly confessed to numerous murders (13) over a 20-year period. Due to the problems of acquiring evidence

for murders committed over such a long time period, Kroll was eventually charged with only eight murders and one attempted murder. In a trial that lasted five months, Kroll was eventually convicted on all counts in April 1982, and sentenced to life imprisonment. But on July 1, 1991, he obtained the ultimate form of early release when he died of a heart attack. One interesting point about his incarceration, however, was that Kroll looked into the possibility of surgical procedures to rid him of his sexual desires. As is the case with many serial killers, it seems that Kroll's murderous habit was hardwired into both his biology and his personality, and as such had no place in society.

Timeline of a Murderer—Known Victims of Joachim Kroll

DATE	VICTIM	AGE	DETAILS
February 8, 1955	Irmgard Strehl	19	Raped, stabbed, and disemboweled; body found in a barn in Lüdinghausen.
1956	Erika Schuleter	12	Abducted, raped, and strangled in the town of Kirchellen.
June 16, 1959	Klara Frieda Tesmer	24	Murdered in fields near Rheinhausen; Heinrich Ott arrested for the crime, and hangs himself in jail.
July 26, 1959	Manuela Knodt	16	Raped and strangled in the City Park of Essen; Kroll removes slices of flesh from her buttocks and thighs.
1962	Barbara Bruder	12	Abducted in Burscheid and murdered; body was never found.
April 23, 1962	Petra Giese	13	Raped and murdered in Dinslaken-Bruckhausen; Vinzenz Kühn is arrested and convicted of the murder.
June 4, 1962	Monika Tafel	12	Murdered in Walsum; slices of flesh cut from her buttocks. Walter Quicker is arrested and released, but later commits suicide.
August 22, 1965	Hermann Schmitz		Murdered as he sits in a car with his girlfriend, Marion Veen, in Duisburg-Großenbaumand; Marion escapes.
September 13, 1966	Ursula Rohling		Murdered in Försterbusch Park near Marl; her boyfriend, Adolf Schickel, is accused of the crime and later commits suicide.
December 22, 1966	Ilona Harke	5	Raped and murdered in Wuppertal; Kroll kills her by drowning her in a ditch.
July 12, 1969	Maria Hettgen	61	Raped and strangled in Hückeswagen.
May 21, 1970	Jutta Rahn	13	Attacked and strangled while walking home from a train station. Peter Schay was arrested and released, but eventually confessed to the crime following pressure from local people.
c. June 1976	Karin Toepfer	10	Raped and strangled in Voerde.
July 3, 1976	Marion Ketter	4	This murder leads to Kroll's arrest.

DENNIS NILSEN

To study the life of Dennis Nilsen is to journey into a chilling, mechanistic pathology. Looking at photos of the man himself, it is hard to conceive how this reticent, mild-mannered civil servant was responsible for the murder of at least 15 men and boys, ostensibly to provide him with a deathly form of company.

Balanced against the other serial killers considered in this book, Dennis Andrew Nilsen did not appear to have an excessively traumatic childhood, although the roots of some of his later tendencies are evident. He was born on November 23, 1945 in Fraserburgh, Scotland, to an ex-Norwegian soldier, Olav Nilsen, and his wife Betty. Life in the Nilsen household was not particularly harmonious—his alcoholic father ended up abandoning Dennis and

◄ Police officers dig for evidence in Dennis Nilsen's garden in Melrose Avenue, London, England. In total, Nilsen committed six murders at the Melrose Avenue address between 1978 and 1981.

Timeline of a Murder

1: Late on the evening of December 30, 1978, Dennis Nilsen meets *Stephen Dean Holmes*, 14, in a London gay bar. He invites him back to his apartment at 195 Melrose Avenue, and Holmes accepts.

2: Back at the apartment, the two of them continue drinking. They eventually climb into bed with each another and fall asleep. Waking in the morning, Nilsen realizes that soon the young man will leave. He determines to kill him to prevent that happening.

3: Nilsen takes his necktie, which is lying on the floor of the bedroom, and wraps it around Holmes' throat. He pulls tight, and Holmes instantly awakens, fighting for his life. They struggle for some time, but eventually Holmes is rendered unconscious.

4: Realizing that Holmes is still alive, Nilsen goes into the kitchen and fills a large plastic bucket full of water. He lifts the unconscious Holmes onto some chairs, then lowers his head into the bucket of water. After several minutes of submersion, Holmes is dead.

5: After recovering from the killing, Nilsen takes the body into the bathroom and washes its hair. He then carries the corpse back into the bedroom and lays it out on his bed.

6: Nilsen indulges in several days of "relationship" with the body of Stephen Holmes, and finally buries him under the floorboards of the apartment.

his mother, and the pair were forced to live at Betty's parents' home. The young Dennis became particularly close to his grandfather, Andrew Whyte. However, that relationship was abruptly terminated when Andrew had a heart attack and died in 1951. Dennis was taken to see his grandfather's body, an experience which, combined with his Roman Catholic family's lectures on the corruption and impurity of the flesh, seems to have left an indelible and formative mark upon Dennis' character.

As a teenager, Dennis appears to have fused sex and death into one. He later testified to enjoying masturbating in front of a mirror while pretending to be a corpse. As yet he showed no signs of cruelty, however. In fact, he was vehemently opposed to any form of cruelty to animals, although as we shall see, such tenderness ultimately did not extend to humans.

FINDING HIS WAY

Finding himself increasingly lonely and alienated from his mother (Betty had four other children, so had scant time for him), at the age of 16 Nilsen opted to join the army. It seemed a curious choice for such a sensitive young man, but by this time he was fully aware of his developing homosexuality and his preference for the company of men. Yet the army did not quench some of the more chilling aspects of his character. He struck up a particularly close friendship with one of his army colleagues. As

part of this friendship, Nilsen even convinced the young man in question to pose as if he were a corpse. Although the relationship was not a homosexual one, Nilsen appears to have been besotted with the young man, and was mortified when he left the army and broke off all contact.

In 1972, after 11 years in the army, Nilsen quit military service and tried his hand in the police force. This career failed after only a year, and he then went to work in a job center in Soho, London. The location was significant. Soho had a thriving gay scene, one that Nilsen was soon enjoying via a string of casual sexual encounters. He eventually built up a more substantial and serious relationship with one David Gallichan, with whom he lived for two years. Eventually the relationship broke down, and Gallichan left (at Nilsen's request) in 1975. Nilsen was now on his own again, left to indulge an aching loneliness and increasingly strange sexual indulgences.

On December 30, 1978, Dennis picked up 14-year-old Stephen Dean Holmes in a London gay bar, and took him back to his garden apartment in Cricklewood. (It should be noted that at the time Nilsen was unlikely to have known that Holmes

▶ **Dennis Nilsen spent a total of 11 years in the British Army. During this time, one of the skills he acquired was butchery, an ability he would later apply to his murder victims.**

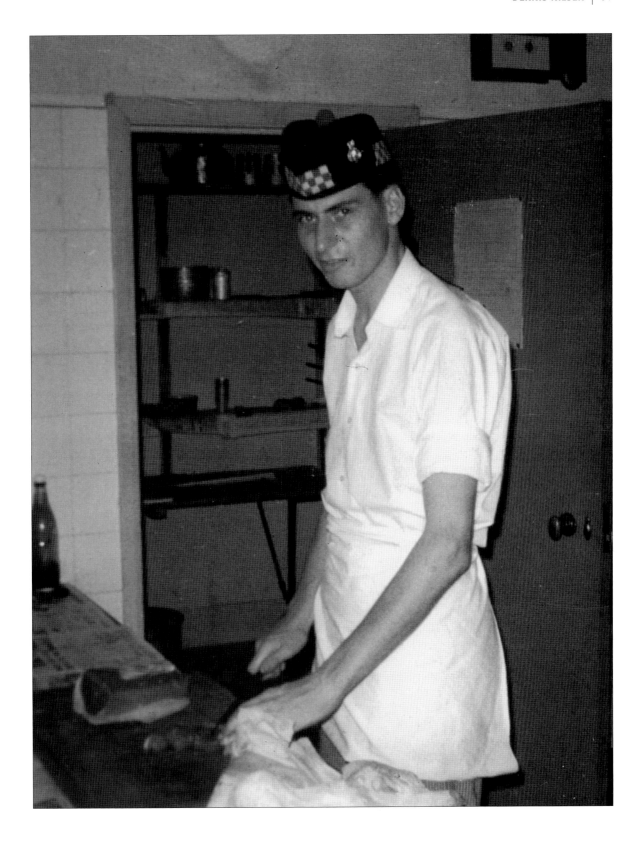

was only 14 years old, as he didn't even know the boy's name.) Later in the evening, when Holmes was sleeping, Nilsen was overpowered by the urge to stop him from ever leaving the apartment. He wrapped a necktie around the boy's throat and strangled him until he was unconscious. Then he submerged Holmes's head in a bucket of water until he was dead.

This was the first of Nilsen's 15 known murders. The postmortem behavior also reveals his utter psychosis. After killing the young man, he then gave the corpse a bath and spent the next few days enacting a bizarre relationship with the body, stroking it and engaging in various sex acts. After a few days, when the body was becoming more unpalatable, he hid it beneath the floorboards in his apartment.

SERIAL KILLER

Nilsen's first murder set the pattern for most of those that were to follow. It would take until December 1979 before he killed again, murdering 23-year-old Canadian student Kenneth Ockendon by strangling him with a headphones cord. Thereafter, he killed men with efficient regularity. By October 1981, he had murdered no fewer than 12 people. As part of his army service, Nilsen had trained as a butcher. He now put his old skills to fresh use, chopping up the victims when he'd finished with them and storing the parts in various locations around his apartment—under the floorboards, in cupboards, down drains, and even burning body parts on bonfires in the backyard. (He would often lay a tire on the bonfire to disguise the hideous smell of burning flesh.)

From what Nilsen subsequently told researchers and psychologists, he wanted to stop what he was doing, but the practice of murder had become deeply engrained. He later said, "I wished I could stop but I could not. I had no other thrill or happiness." In October 1981 he moved to a new apartment, in Muswell Hill. This apartment was in the attic of the building, and part of him hoped that the challenges of body disposal in the new seting

▶ 23 Cranley Gardens, Muswell Hill, north London. Here Nilsen murdered three men between March 1982 and January 1983. It was the blocked drains here that led to Nilsen's eventual arrest.

would prevent his habit from expressing itself. He largely targeted lonely, drifting young men passing through the capital, so he had managed to stay well ahead of the London police. Most of the victims simply went into the Metropolitan Police's already bulging missing persons files.

Nilsen was soon back to his old ways. In November 1981 he attempted to murder a London student, although on this occasion he did not succeed. The student in question, his memory of the previous night blotted out by alcohol, even went to the doctor the following day. The doctor revealed that he had probably been strangled, but the young man's fear of revealing his homosexuality to police prevented him from reporting the incident. Similarly, Nilsen failed in his attempt to strangle and drown another man shortly afterward; again this man failed to report the incident, largely

Timeline of a Murderer—Known Victims of Dennis Nilsen

DATE	VICTIM	AGE	DETAILS
December 30, 1978	Stephen Dean Holmes	14	Nilsen strangles and drowns his victim at 195 Melrose Avenue, Cricklewood, London, having picked him up in a gay bar.
December 3, 1979	Kenneth Ockendon	23	Nilsen murders the Canadian student with a headphones cord, having met him in a London pub.
May 17, 1980	Martyn Duffey	16	Martyn Duffey was a runaway from Birkenhead. He was strangled then drowned in Nilsen's kitchen sink.
August 1980	Billy Sutherland	26	Nilsen strangles the 26-year-old with his bare hands.
August 1980–September 1981			At points throughout this period, Nilsen murders another seven men, all of them unidentified.
September 18, 1981	Malcom Barlow	24	The 24-year-old became the last of Nilsen's victims to be murdered at Melrose Avenue.
March 1982	John Howlett	n/a	Nilsen met John Howlett in a local pub and he became the first victim in Nilsen's Muswell Hill home.
September 1982	Graham Allen	n/a	Nilsen kills this homeless man, strangling him after he prepared him something to eat.
January 26, 1983	Stephen Sinclair	20	Nilsen kills his final victim and it is his remains that lead the police to the scene of the crime.

because alcohol and the effects of the strangulation had obliterated his memory.

In March 1982, however, Nilsen claimed his first victim in his new home, killing one John Howlett following a vicious struggle. He then chopped up the body and distributed some of the parts around the flat, while flushing others down the toilet. Nilsen had killed twice more by the end of January 1983, disposing of the bodies in a similar manner. He would also boil body parts, including entire heads, in pans on the stove to remove the flesh, which he then flushed down the toilet along with pieces of chopped-up entrails. His apartment was filled with the diabolical smell of death. The grim practicalities of this body disposal would be his undoing.

GRUESOME DISCOVERY

In February 1983, a drain clearing company was called to Nilsen's apartment block following complaints about blocked drains from another tenant. The workman assembled his cleaning rods and set about trying to clear what was evidently a serious blockage. As he worked on the drain, he saw that the source of the problem, which was traced to Nilsen's flat, was large amounts of a flesh-like substance interspersed with what seemed to be small human bones. The engineer called his supervisor, and between them they began to suspect the unthinkable. They called the police. Detective Chief Inspector Peter Jay and two other officers were called to the scene, and when Nilsen returned home from work they went up to his apartment to confront him.

Jay tested Nilsen for a response by saying that they had possibly found human remains in the drainage system. Coolly, Dennis simply remarked "How awful." Quickly, Jay upped the ante, asking him directly, "Don't mess about. Where's the rest of the body?" With the same impassive attitude,

Nilsen admitted that the parts of many bodies were stored in plastic bags in his cupboard. Jay and the other officers moved inside the apartment, nearly gagging on the overwhelming stench of death. As the officers saw the horrors around them, Nilsen was arrested immediately. In the police car, he confessed that he had killed some "15 or 16" people.

Once back at the station, Nilsen really opened up. Over the course of 30 hours of police questioning, he confessed to all the murders in turn, elaborating on his methods of both killing and disposal. He gave his confessions calmly and seemingly with neither emotion nor regret. Each new scrap of detail provided the police with fresh information to continue their hunt for bodies and missing persons. Later, however, when his lawyers showed him photographs from the scenes of his crimes, he became nauseous at what he'd done. As if wanting to guarantee his conviction, Nilsen even produced 50 notebooks containing details of murders he committed, including what he called "sad sketches"—drawings of his victims in various attitudes of death.

Naturally, with such evidence at the court's disposal, the question of Nilsen's guilt was not up for discussion. Instead, the essence of the trial, when it began on October 24, 1983, was the battle between a prosecution who claimed that he was of sound mind when he committed the six murders and two attempted murders with which he was charged, versus a defense whose case rested on arguing for diminished responsibility through mental abnormality. The case became a particular confusing one for the jury, as each side shipped in different psychiatrists as expert witnesses, who produced analyses often far beyond the understanding of the court. During his summing-up, however, the judge percolated the evidence down to the understandable issues of Nilsen's evil and clear-minded disposition, and on November 4, a majority verdict found him guilty on all counts. He was sentenced to life imprisonment.

As an interesting endnote to Nilsen's life, his time in prison has included a certain amount of activism on his part, launching judicial protests over issues such as his right to access gay pornography and his desire to publish his own autobiography, titled *The History of a Drowning Boy*.

▼ Dennis Nilson committed murder with simple tools. The tie/rope combination was used to strangle the victims, who were then cut up with the butcher's knife, on the cutting board shown. The instrument at top right is a knife sharpener.

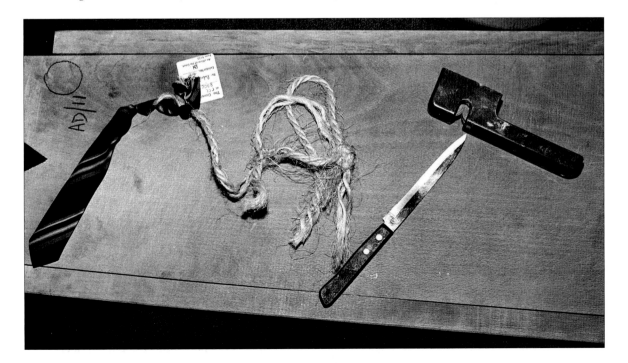

EDMUND KEMPER

The case of Edmund Kemper is distinctive among the grim lives of serial killers contained in this book, but not because of the number of people he killed, which was 10 in total. Rather, Kemper stands out not only as someone who murdered several members of his own family, including his mother and grandparents, but also because his grotesque crimes were eventually stopped by his giving himself up to police voluntarily and confessing to everything.

Born on December 18, 1948, in Burbank, California, Edmund Emil Kemper was in many ways the tragic product of a broken home. His parents' marriage was dissolving around him, and they separated when he was only nine years old. The separation was particularly traumatic for the young boy, who missed his father terribly. His mother also isolated him within the household, creating a room in the basement away

◄ Edmund Kemper (left) is escorted into court in Santa Cruz, California, on April 30, 1973. Kemper is fairly unusual in the ranks of serial killers, as he eventually turned himself in to the police and openly confessed.

Timeline of a Murder

The following is based on Kemper's own confessions:

1: May 7, 1972. *Mary Anne Pesce* and *Anita Luchessa*, both 18, are hitchhiking from Fresno to Stanford University, a journey of 168 miles (270km). Kemper picks them up in his Ford Galaxie when they are about an hour from their destination. He later noted that both girls seemed very naive, despite attempting to appear streetwise.

2: A short distance into the journey, Kemper drives his car off the road onto a dirt track, and tells the girls that he is going to rape them. The girls begin to panic, but Kemper handcuffs Pesce to the back seat of the car, and drags Luchessa around the rear of the vehicle and forces her into the trunk.

3: Kemper returns to the interior of the vehicle, pulls out a knife and stabs Pesce in the back, although the wound is not fatal. He also unsuccessfully tries to smother her. There is a violent struggle, and Kemper only succeeds in killing the young woman when he slits her throat. He then returns to the trunk, where he murders Luchessa in a similar fashion.

4: Kemper wraps the two bodies in blankets and places them in the trunk of the car. He drives them back to his apartment, on the way being stopped by a police officer and cautioned for a broken taillight. Once back at the apartment, he takes the bodies up to his bedroom, where he photographs and dismembers the corpses, having sex with various body parts.

5: Kemper takes the body parts out around the local wilderness, sexually abusing some of them once again before disposing of them.

from her and his two sisters, possibly through genuine fear of his actions. Alone with his thoughts, it appears from later behavior that Kemper had already begun to develop a pathological aggression toward women.

There were many disturbing signs that Edmund Kemper was not developing as a normal child should. He murdered two family cats, one with a machete, and would cut the heads off his sisters' dolls. At the age of 10, in response to his sister's teasing comments about his wanting to kiss an attractive schoolteacher, he said "If I kiss her I would have to kill her first." When he was 15 he left home and spent a short period with his father and stepmother in Los Angeles, but the move didn't work out and he ended up living with his grandparents, Maude and Edmund Kemper.

Taking in the disturbed young man would have fatal consequences for the elderly couple. On August 27, 1964, he had an argument with Maude Kemper in the kitchen of their home. Taking a small-caliber hunting rifle, he then shot his grandmother three times, once in the head and twice in the back, killing her. At that moment his grandfather also arrived back at the house, pulling up in the car outside. Kemper went to the window, took aim, and shot his grandfather dead on the spot. Having committed a double murder, Kemper first phoned his mother and then the police, to whom he confessed what he had done. He told them that he had shot his grandmother just to see what it felt like.

It was clear that Edmund Kemper was in poor mental health. Psychiatric evaluation classified him as a paranoid schizophrenic, and he was eventually incarcerated in the Atascadero State Hospital for the Criminally Insane. During his time there, hospital authorities were impressed with his exceptional IQ and seeming improvements in behavior, and following extensive treatment he was released back into the community in 1969, aged 21.

A DESIRE TO KILL

Once in the outside world again, Kemper went to stay with his mother, who now lived in Santa Cruz, California. This was the late 1960s, and Kemper did not fit in well with the counterculture style that dominated the southwestern United States. For a start, he was a visually intimidating individual—he eventually grew to 6ft 9in (2.05m) tall. He also struggled to achieve his chosen career; he wanted to be a police officer, but was eventually stuck in employment as a laborer with the California Division of Highways.

Around the early 1970s, Kemper began to pick up female hitchhikers, of whom there were many traveling around California at this time. He perfected a friendly and open-mannered approach to gain their trust, and dozens of girls were transported perfectly safely in his yellow Ford Galaxie. Yet what seemed to be a simple act of helpfulness was actually masking something far more sinister.

On May 7, 1972, Kemper picked up two young women, Mary Ann Pesce and Anita Luchessa, both aged 18 and hitchhiking from Fresno to Stanford University. They would not reach their destination. At some point in the journey, Kemper slaughtered both women, before taking their corpses back to his apartment, photographing and sexually molesting them, then dumping them in the wilderness (see "Timeline of a Murder"). Something had obviously snapped in his character, and over the next eight years he would murder six more times, on each occasion revisiting his grotesque pattern of abduction, murder, necrophilia, and mutilation.

BEYOND BELIEF

The sickening nature of the Kemper murders stretches the limits of our comprehension. His second victim was 15-year-old Aiko Koo. Having again picked her up while she was hitchhiking, he then unsuccessfully attempted to suffocate her with his hands, before strangling her and again taking her back his apartment to dismember and abuse at his leisure. It is tragic to note that just two days later Kemper went before a parole board, who actually judged him rehabilitated and safe to be in the community. Even as the board was coming to that assessment, in Kemper's car outside was the decapitated head of Aiko Koo, Kemper having already disposed of her other body parts.

There was now a break of four months between murders, but on January 8, 1973 he killed again, this time 19-year-old student Cindy Schall. By this time, Kemper was back living with his mother, and her house became the primary venue for her son's horrible dismemberment and sex rituals.

On February 5, Kemper went out to kill again, this time fueled by the rage from an earlier argument with his mother. He picked up two students, Rosalind Thorpe (24) and Alison Liu (23), and actually shot them both while he was driving.

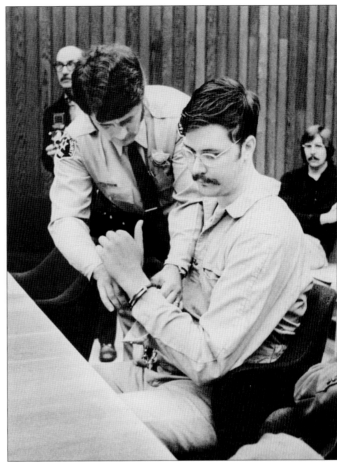

▲ A court official removes handcuffs from Edmund Kemper prior to the reading of the trial verdict. The jury found Kemper guilty on eight counts of first-degree murder, a verdict that they reached after five and a half hours of deliberation.

Afterwards he even drove through a university checkpoint, but bluffed his way past the security guard by saying that that the two dead or dying girls were actually just drunk.

FINAL ACTS

Then, on April 20, 1973, Edmund Kemper's killing spree came to its logical climax. In the early hours of the morning, he went into his mother's bedroom and beat her to death with a claw hammer. In his later confession, he said that this act was emotionally traumatic, but he still had enough hatred to remove her head, and after

◄ Aiko Koo, 15, was murdered by Kemper on September 14, 1972 after he had picked her up as she was hitchhiking. The unfortunate girl's head was buried in Kemper's mother's backyard.

shouting at it he then used it as a dartboard. Compounding the killing of his mother, he then invited over his mother's friend, Sally Hallett, who was strangled and beheaded when she arrived for dinner.

It seemed that these final killings emotionally exhausted what little humanity remained in Edmund Kemper. The very next day, having driven some 1500 miles (2414km) to Pueblo, Colorado, he called the Santa Cruz police department and confessed everything.

Once in police custody, Kemper gave details of all the eight murders he had committed since 1972. The subsequent trial revolved around assessments of his mental health, but in April 1973 he was found guilty of eight counts of first-degree murder and was sentenced to life imprisonment. Although eligible for parole from 1980, he has to date been denied release on at least six occasions. Given the gravity and manner of his crimes, this is hardly surprising.

Timeline of a Murderer—Known Victims of Edmund Kemper

DATE	VICTIM	AGE	DETAILS
August 27, 1964	Edmund Kemper	72	Edmund's grandparents, shot with a rifle that his
	Maud Kemper	66	grandfather had bought him the previous Christmas.
May 7, 1972	Mary Anne Pesce	18	Both killed in Alameda, California, after being picked up
	Anita Luchessa	18	hitchhiking; the bodies were dismembered, used for sexual purposes, and dumped in the wilderness.
September 14, 1972	Aiko Koo	15	Strangled to death by the side of the road after being picked up hitchhiking; Kemper raped and dismembered the body and buried Koo's head in his mother's backyard.
January 8, 1973	Cindy Schall	19	Picked up from the Cabrillo College campus and executed in an isolated area; Kemper dismembered the body in his mother's bathtub.
February 5, 1973	Rosalind Thorpe	24	Both picked up on the UC Santa Cruz campus and shot while
	Alison Liu	23	Kemper was driving; again, he dismembered the bodies in his mother's house.
April 20, 1973	Clarnell Strandberg Kemper	52	Clarnell was beaten to death in the early hours of the
	Sally Hallett	59	morning with a claw hammer; Hallett was then lured into visiting the house, where she was strangled to death. Both bodies were severely mutilated.

RICHARD RAMIREZ

The horrifying tale of Richard Ramirez is one of a young man who explicitly embraced evil as a life philosophy. Only 25 years old by the time he was apprehended in 1985, he had taken a total of 14 lives, seemingly without compunction. In fact, when sentenced to death, he simply shrugged away the sentence, saying "Big deal. Death always went with the territory. See you in Disneyland."

Richard Ramirez came from the town of El Paso on the Texas–Mexican border, where he was born on February 28, 1960, the son of Mexican immigrants Julian and Mercedes. He had a fairly tough childhood under a very strict father—he would sometimes sleep in a local cemetery to avoid his father's wrath. Yet what seems to be a critical moment in his psychological development came when he started

◀ Richard Ramirez presented a self-consciously evil persona during his trial in 1988–89. The case nevertheless turned into one of the longest trials in U.S. legal history, lasting more than a year.

Timeline of a Murder

1: Evening of March 17, 1985, Rosemead, California. *Maria Hernandez*, 22, parks her car in the garage of the condominium she shares with her roommate, *Dayle Okazaki*, 24. As she leaves the garage she is approached by a man, Richard Ramirez, dressed in black and with a baseball cap pulled down low over his face.

2: As the man comes closer, Hernandez sees that he has a gun. She lifts her hands to her face as the man raises the gun and fires. The bullet strikes the keys and her hand, but she falls to the floor as if dead. Ramirez shoves her body to one side and goes inside the condominium.

3: Ramirez works his way through the condominium, and finds Okazaki in the kitchen. He shoots her through the head at close range, killing her, and then pulls up her blouse.

4: Exiting the condominium, Ramirez sees Hernandez alive and moving about. He raises the gun but she asks him not to shoot. Ramirez lowers the gun and walks away.

5: Hernandez goes into the condominium, where she discovers the body of her roommate.

spending more time with his cousin Mike, who in 1972 was only recently back from combat service in Vietnam. Mike exposed Richard to graphic photographs of killing and sexual violence. One photograph depicted Mike receiving oral sex from a woman at gunpoint, while the next photograph showed the same woman's severed head. Rather than revolting him, these images seem to have struck something of a sexual chord in the young man. Furthermore, in May 1973 he personally witnessed Mike shoot his wife in the face, killing her. So by the time he was 13, Richard Ramirez had some very unhealthy seeds planted in his character.

The rest of Richard's teenage years saw a steady deterioration in character and lifestyle. He learned some techniques of petty crime, such as how to break into houses, and spent more and more time stoned on dope or hallucinogens. He also developed an interest in hunting, going out with his gun to track down small mammals and birds. Inevitably he found himself in trouble with the law, a problem that increased when he moved to Los Angeles in 1978, where he had some family. (He had dropped out of high school by this time.) During his late teens and early twenties he was arrested numerous times, mainly for charges relating to burglary and theft. He became a delinquent in appearance, with a mouthful of rotted teeth from overindulgence in fizzy drinks and junk food. It was hard to see how he could stoop much lower, but he did.

SATAN'S CHILD
When he was 18, Richard Ramirez began to practice Satan worship. Rather than being a teenage

act of defiance, this attraction toward self-conscious evil seemed genuine, and led to horrific outcomes. Just how horrific became clear on the night of June 28, 1984. Using his skills as a burglar, he broke into the home of 79-year-old Jennie Vincow and stabbed her to death in her own bed after sexually assaulting her. This was only the beginning of his killing spree, although he would wait until March 17, 1985 before claiming his next victims. On this day, he shot two women around their own condo (see "Timeline of a Murder"), one of whom survived while the other died of her injuries. The very same night, he shot Tsai-Lian Yu, 30, dragging her from her car near Monterey Park and shooting her twice in the chest. As if this orgy of killing wasn't enough, just 10 days later he killed the owner of a pizza store and his wife. The wife's body was terribly mutilated, including stud marks all over her face and body; her eyes had been cut out. Most of these injuries occurred, thankfully, after the two people had been shot dead.

The fact was that in the space of nine months, Richard Ramirez had gone from being a habitual petty criminal to a serial killer with five murders under his belt.

TARGETING COUPLES
One sadly interesting feature of Ramirez's murderous career was that he increasingly focused his attentions upon couples rather than individuals. Such is unusual—attacking two people involves a much greater risk of being overpowered and caught, or being injured in the confrontation. Nevertheless, Ramirez was not dissuaded, and

relied on the power of firearms and surprise to retain the advantage.

The next attack came on May 14, 1985, when he shot 66-year-old William Doi in his home, then proceeded to rape his elderly wife. The dying Mr. Doi, however, had enough strength to make a 911 call, and the timely arrival of the police saved his wife, but not him, from death. Ramirez escaped, although Lillian Doi managed to provide the police with the first clear description of the serial killer. Shortly afterward, on May 29, Ramirez beat two women, both in their 80s, with a hammer, killing one of them and carving a pentagram on the dead woman's thigh. (Another pentagram was etched into the wall of the room.) Just a day later, Ramirez raped and sodomized a 41-year-old woman, having locked her 12-year-old son in the closet. For reasons unknown, he then released the boy, tied the pair together, and left the scene.

The intense rhythm of Ramirez's blood lust had a terrifying regularity, and some diversity. In June 1985, for example, he raped a six-year-old girl and the next day slit a young woman's throat. The following July, he killed another five people (three in one day) and seriously injured several others; in one of his attacks, he raped an eight-year-old boy after murdering his father and raping his mother. Still he was not finished. On August 6, he awoke Christopher Peterson and his wife Virginia, and shot

▼ Despite being on death row, Ramirez managed to strike up a relationship with one Doreen Lioy, to whom he was married in San Quentin Prison on Thursday October 3, 1996.

both of them in the head, although miraculously they survived. Another couple, Ahmed Zia, 35, and his wife Suu Kyi were not so lucky—two days after the Petersen shootings Ramirez shot Ahmed dead and then put his wife through a grotesque and prolonged sexual assault.

DATABASE

By early August it was patently clear to both the Los Angeles police and the public that a serial killer was committing all these attacks and murders. The fact that this was the work of the same man was evident by the pattern to the attacks, which on couples typically involved killing the man first then subjecting the woman to sexual assault, before in effect "signing" his work through carving pentagrams either on the bodies or on other physical features around the victims' home. Because the attacks were conducted at night, the killer was nicknamed the "Night Stalker," and the police set up a taskforce to attempt to catch him.

Feeling the heat, but not dissuaded from murder, Ramirez now switched his attentions to San Francisco. On the night of August 17, Ramirez allegedly (he would not be charged with their

▼ **A police artist's impression of Ramirez. A photo issued later to the press led to Ramirez's capture, when members of the public recognized him from the photo and overpowered him in a violent struggle.**

murders) broke into the home of Peter and Barbara Pan and shot them both, carving his signature pentagram on the wall.

On August 25, Richard Ramirez committed his final killing. He broke into the home of Bill Carns, 29, and his fiancée, Inez Erickson. He shot Carns in the head, killing him, then set about raping Inez and forcing her to swear a love for Satan. He then tied her up and fled, but as he was fleeing witnesses managed to note the license plate of the car he was driving. It was the simple, effective evidence that the police needed. The car, a Toyota station wagon, was later discovered abandoned, but the police managed to lift a fingerprint. When that fingerprint was fed into the newly updated Sacramento fingerprint database, it brought up a match for Richard Ramirez, his prints having been logged from previous arrests. Realizing that they had to stop this man fast, the police issued a photo to the Los Angeles press, a fact that Ramirez discovered when he went into a drugstore in east LA and saw his own face looming out from the front pages of the newspapers. Identified by local crowds, he was only saved from being lynched by the arrival of the police.

During the trial of Richard Ramirez, he came across as a virtually demonic figure. He raised a hand to press photographers, clearly showing the pentagram he had drawn on the palm, and on other occasions he held his fingers to the side of his head as if he were a demon. It was not a winning performance for a man who had entered a not guilty plea, although that plea was largely the result of defense team tactics. Eventually, on September 20, 1989, he was found guilty on 13 counts of murder plus 30 other offences (many more individuals had been attacked by Ramirez and survived). He was sentenced to death,

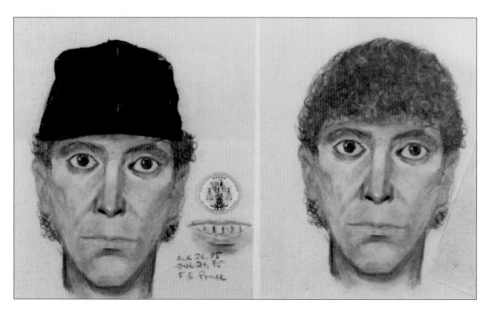

and was dispatched to San Quentin prison, where he remains to this day on death row. In a bizarre aside, during and after the trial he attracted something of a cult following from evidently unbalanced females. In fact, he even married one, Doreen Lioy, in prison in October 1996.

Timeline of a Murderer—Known Victims of Richard Ramirez

DATE	VICTIM	AGE	DETAILS
June 28, 1984	Jennie Vincow	79	Ramirez broke into her house, then stabbed Jennie and slit her throat; he had sex with the corpse before leaving.
March 17, 1985	Dayle Okazaki	34	(see p94 "Timeline of a Murder").
March 17, 1985	Tsai-Lian Yu	30	Ramirez pulls her from her car and shoots her; she dies in the ambulance. He attacked and sexually abused an eight-year-old girl three days after this incident.
March 27, 1985	Vincent Zazarra Maxine Zazarra	64 44	Vincent and his wife Maxine are shot dead; Maxine's body is heavily mutilated, including a T-shape carved on her left breast; bullets used in the killings matched those of earlier Ramirez murders.
May 14, 1985	William Doi	66	Ramirez shot William, who later died of his wounds, and raped his wife Lillian, 63; William managed to phone 911, an act that prevented Ramirez from killing Lillian.
May 29, 1985	Malvia Keller	83	Beaten with a hammer along with her invalid sister, Blanche Wolfe, 80; Malvia dies, but Blanche survives.
June 27, 1985	Patty Higgins	32	Beaten and her throat slit.
July 2, 1985	Mary Louise Cannon	75	Beaten and her throat slit.
July 7, 1985	Joyce Lucille Nelson	61	Beaten to death.
July 20, 1985	Maxson Kneiding Lela Kneiding	66 66	Maxson and his wife Lela were shot and their corpses mutilated with a machete, the first time Ramirez had used this weapon in a murder.
July 20, 1985	Chitat Assawahem	31	Chitat was shot dead and his wife Sakima, 29, was beaten then forced to perform oral sex; he also sodomized the couple's eight-year-old son.
August 8, 1985	Ahmed Zia	35	Ahmed was shot dead and his wife, Suu Kyi, 28, suffered a sustained sexual assault.
August 17, 1985	Peter Pan	66	Shot and killed; his wife survived but was left disabled from the incident; Ramirez was not charged with this murder.
August 25, 1985	Bill Carns	29	Bill was shot dead, then Ramirez sexually assaulted his fiancée, Inez Erickson, 27.

JEFFREY DAHMER

Many serial killers have murdered more people than Jeffery Dahmer. Compared to an Andrei Chikatilo or a Harold Shipman, for example, his tally of 17 people appears almost modest, although still a chilling number. And yet Dahmer stands out largely because of the manner in which he killed people. Few serial killers go to the inventive and gruesome lengths explored by Dahmer, and he remains one of the most sickening individuals in the history of serial killers.

S omething seemed wrong with Jeffrey Dahmer from his earliest years. He was born on May 21, 1960 in Milwaukee, Wisconsin, to Lionel and Joyce Dahmer. For the first two years at least, Jeffrey seemed a relatively content and happy child, although as he grew older he became increasingly aware of his parents' unhappy marriage, which resulted in constant arguments and

◀ Family members of some the victims of Jeffrey Dahmer talk to the press outside the courtroom during the 1992 trial. The badges display photographs of their murdered relatives.

fighting. By the age of six they had moved into separate bedrooms, and the young boy had already begun a descent into a lonely and disturbing world.

Early indicators that all was not well with the boy came around the age of seven. He gave a bowl of tadpoles to one of his teachers as an affectionate present. The teacher then passed the tadpoles on to one of Dahmer's few friends, Lee, and in retribution Jeffrey killed the tadpoles with engine oil. This act was just the beginning of a ghastly relationship to animals. By the age of eight he was experimenting on small animals ranging from fish and frogs to cats. He later took to patrolling the roads looking out for roadkill, then taking the corpses back home and stripping them down to skeletons.

Timeline of a Murderer—Known Victims of Jeffrey Dahmer

DATE	VICTIM	AGE	DETAILS
June 18, 1978	Stephen Hicks	19	Killed with a barbell and dismembered.
September 15, 1987	Steven Tourmi	c. 25	Murdered in the Ambassador Hotel and transported in a suitcase back to Dahmer's grandmother's house for dismemberment.
January 1988	James 'Jamie' Doxtator	14	Drugged with sleeping pills and strangled; remains stuffed in the trash.
March 24, 1988	Richard Guerrero	25	Dahmer has sex with Guerrero's corpse before disposing of it.
March 29, 1989	Anthony Sears	24	Offered money by Dahmer to take explicit photos; after his murder Dahmer boils Sears' head and keeps the skull.
June 1990	Eddie Smith	6	Drugged and murdered at Dahmer's apartment.
July 1990	Ricky Beeks	27	Dahmer keeps Beeks' skull after the murder.
September 3, 1990	Ernest Miller	23	Dahmer keeps Miller's entire skeleton and later eats his biceps.
September 24, 1990	David Thomas	22	Photographed while the murder is taking place.
February 17, 1991	Curtis Straughter	19	Skull retained following the murder.
April 7, 1991	Errol Lindsey	19	Again, Dahmer retains the head.
May 24, 1991	Tony Hughes	31	A deaf-mute victim; Dahmer retains the head.
May 27, 1991	Konerak Sinthasomphone	14	Dahmer's youngest known victim.
June 30, 1991	Matt Turner	20	His head is placed in Dahmer's freezer.
July 5, 1991	Jeremiah Weinberger	23	Head kept in the freezer.
July 12, 1991	Oliver Lacy	24	Both his head and his heart are kept in the refrigerator (these are two of the first things officers later find in Dahmer's apartment).
July 19, 1991	Joseph Bradehoft	25	His head is kept in the freezer, while his other body parts are dissolved in acid.

▲ The trial of Jeffrey Dahmer presented constant evidence of his depravity. Yet although Dahmer eventually adopted a position of guilty but insane, the jury rejected the plea of insanity, and he was eventually sentenced to more than 900 years in prison.

By the time Dahmer was in high school, things had deteriorated even more. At the age of 13 he lay the foundations of a lifelong alcoholism, and gradually his behavior became more isolating and aggressive. He would pretend to have epileptic fits in the school corridors, or bleat like a sheep while in class. By his late teens he even used to draw chalk body outlines on the classroom floor, and confessed to having fantasies about sex with a corpse. Near his house, some boys walking through the local woods discovered a decapitated dog, the head mounted on a stake and the body skinned and nailed to a tree. Naturally enough, Dahmer soon had no friends to call on.

THE NEXT STEP

In 1978, Dahmer's emerging depravity began an even darker evolution. It was the year in which his parents finally divorced, and the young man often found himself alone in the family home with little to occupy his time. He was homosexual in orientation, having had his first homosexual experience at the age of 14. At this stage, his sexuality and his fascination with death began to coalesce.

On June 18, 1978, Dahmer picked up a local hitchhiker—Stephen Hicks, 19—and invited him back to his house. They became drunk together and had sex. Yet as Hicks went to leave, Dahmer grabbed a barbell and crushed his skull, killing him instantly. He pulled the body underneath the

Timeline of a Murder

1: May 26, 1991. In the late evening, Jeffrey Dahmer offers money to 14-year-old Laotian boy *Konerak Sinthasomphone*, asking him to come back to his apartment. The boy agrees.

2: Back at the apartment, Dahmer strips the boy and sexually assaults him, then gives him a powerful sedative. Dahmer temporarily leaves the apartment while Konerak struggles against unconsciousness. Konerak manages to get to his feet and leaves the apartment, staggering around naked and showing clear signs of sexual assault.

3: Just before 2:00 A.M. on May 27, Sandra Smith (18) and Nicole Childress (18) come across the disoriented young man. Paramedics are called, and then two police officers arrive. Dahmer also returns to the scene and begins to argue with the girls and the police officers.

4: Dahmer convinces the officers that the young man is his 19-year-old boyfriend, who has simply been drinking too much. The girls protest, saying that at one point they had seen Konerak struggling with Dahmer in the street.

5: Believing Dahmer's version of events, the two officers escort him and Konerak back to his apartment. They noticed a bad smell inside—a three-day-old corpse was rotting in the bedroom—but nothing else untoward. They leave Konerak alone in the apartment with Dahmer.

6: Shortly after the officers leave, Dahmer murders and dismembers Konerak.

house into the crawl space, where he set about cutting it up with a kitchen knife and putting the bits in plastic bags. He also later smashed up the bones with a hammer, and scattered them in surrounding woodland.

Having committed his first murder, Dahmer still seems to have attempted to build something approaching a normal life. Later in 1978, he enrolled in Ohio State University, but dropped out by the end of the year as his alcoholism took over. He then, at his father's insistence, joined the U.S. Army, eventually becoming a combat medic. In hindsight, his choice of army specialty seems almost laughable, but it has been noted that during Dahmer's posting to West Germany, a total of five unsolved mutilation murders occurred in the local area. Given Dahmer's instability, it is little wonder that the army eventually discharged him in March 1981. He went first to Florida, then to live with his grandmother in West Allis, Wisconsin, working through a series of dead-end jobs. Although he even began attending church, it was at this stage that he became a true serial killer.

On September 16, 1987, Dahmer woke up in a room in the Ambassador Hotel, Wisconsin. Another first thing he noticed was the corpse of Steven Tourmi, the man who just the night before Dahmer had picked up in a local gay bar. Blood was oozing from the corpse's mouth. Although he had no recollection of what had occurred, Dahmer nevertheless had the presence of mind to go out and purchase a suitcase, into which he stuffed the body. He then called a cab and took the corpse back to his grandmother's house, where he chopped up the body, put the pieces in plastic bags and disposed of them.

KILLING SPREE

The Tourmi murder seems to have triggered the true killer inside Jeffrey Dahmer. His next victim, in January 1988, was 14-year-old James Doxtator, whom he picked up outside the same gay club (Club 219) and took back to his grandmother's house. Following sex, Dahmer then strangled the boy and performed his usual ritual of dismemberment. Then came the killing of Richard Guerrero, 25, on March 24, 1988. Dahmer again followed his now familiar modus operandi, but with a disturbing twist—before dismembering the lifeless man, he had sex with the corpse.

By this stage, Dahmer was not entirely unknown to the local law enforcement community. In September 1986 he had been arrested for masturbating in front of two 12-year-old boys, for which he received one year's probation. In September 1988, he raised his profile a little more. He coaxed a 14-year-old Laotian boy back to his new apartment on 808 North 24th Street—he had moved out of his grandmother's house a few days earlier. He fondled the boy and took explicit pictures, but his attempts to drug him to sleep did not work, and the boy went home to tell his parents what had happened. Dahmer was immediately arrested, charged with child exploitation and second-degree sexual assault, and having been freed on bail was scheduled to go to trial in May 1989.

Both Dahmer's release and the late scheduling of his trial date had fatal consequences for another man, Anthony Sears, 24. He was murdered on March 29—this time Dahmer not only had sex with the corpse, but also boiled Sears' head to remove the flesh, then painted the skull gray.

On May 24, 1989, Dahmer was sentenced to eight years' imprisonment for his assault on the Laotian boy. He would serve only 10 months on account of good behavior, although unknown to the authorities that behavior included sexually assaulting a man with a candlestick when he was given a 12-hour pass to go home for Thanksgiving. Following his release in May 1990, he moved into 924 25th Street, where he resumed his murderous career with greater tempo. During the remainder of the year he killed another four men, and demonstrated new fetishes—he even began indulging in cannibalism, eating the biceps of one of his victims. Dahmer also bought barrels of acid to dissolve human flesh.

In 1991 he chalked up another eight victims as his appetite grew ever more insatiable. He stored entire skeletons and heads in the freezer, and kept

numerous other body parts, including sexual organs, in various receptacles around his apartment. (His bedroom drawers were, for example, stuffed with organs, and genitals were later found in a lobster pot.) On occasions he drilled holes into the skulls of his victims, pouring acid into the holes in attempt to create sexual "zombies." The place reeked of death. During this killing spree, Dahmer came close to being arrested in the act of one of his killings, when 14-year-old Konerak Sinthasomphone was found outside Dahmer's apartment, drugged and bleeding. The police were called, but Dahmer convinced them that nothing more than a lovers' tiff had taken place. The police left, and Sinthasomphone was murdered.

UNDENIABLE GUILT

In late July 1991, Dahmer attempted to repeat his killing ritual with 31-year-old Tracy Edwards. Back at the apartment, Dahmer attempted to handcuff Edwards, but the man escaped and flagged down a passing police patrol car. The officers warily went to Dahmer's apartment, and gained access. Inside the apartment they found evidence of unspeakable atrocities, and quickly wrestled Dahmer to the floor and arrested him.

The horrifying mass of evidence found in the apartment, and eventually from elsewhere, took time to percolate through the system, but eventually Dahmer was charged with 15 counts of murder. He had by this time adopted a policy of pleading guilty but insane, a plea that appears entirely reasonable given the terrifying nature of his crimes. He was sentenced to 941 years in jail in February 1992, and was sent to the Columbia Correctional Institution in Portage, Wisconsin. As an avowed hater of African-Americans, Dahmer had a rough time in prison, being assaulted on several occasions. Finally, on November 28, 1994, he was beaten to death by convicted murderer Christopher Scarver.

◀ A list of some of the victims of Jeffrey Dahmer hangs in the courtroom during his trial. As it indicates, 1991 was Dahmer's most prolific year for killing, murdering eight people in February–July.

EXTERIOR OF THE GATE

JACK THE RIPPER

The case of Jack the Ripper has gripped public imagination since the late nineteenth century. Something about this unsolved series of murders triggers both disquiet and fascination, partly through speculation as to the identity of the murderer—theories range from Jewish barbers through to members of the Royal Family. Yet whatever the intellectual interest in Jack the Ripper, the horror of his crimes is not to be denied.

The story of Jack the Ripper begins with a body, that of Mary Ann Nichols. Nichols was one of the legions of prostitutes who worked London's East End in the late nineteenth century, a vulnerable profession at the best of times. On August 31, 1888, Nichols's corpse was discovered lying in Buck's Row, Whitechapel. Murdered prostitutes were not an uncommon find, but what shocked the police was the sheer violence

◀ A contemporary artwork depicts the discovery of one of Jack the Ripper's victims. The actual number of victims credited to the Ripper is hotly disputed, but five "canonical" victims have been established.

▲ The ninetenth-century media was obsessed with Jack the Ripper. Some newspapers sensationalized every killing, while others presented the Ripper as a product of general social neglect in urban Britain.

Timeline of a Murder

1: Saturday September 8, 1888, 12:10 A.M. *Annie Chapman* drinks a pint of beer with a fellow lodger at Crossingham's Lodging House at 35 Dorset Street, Spitalfields. She then goes out about 1 A.M.

2: 1:35 A.M. Annie Chapman returns to the lodgings and eats a baked potato in her room. She discusses payment of bed money with the night watchman, John Evans, then goes out to work on the streets.

3: 5:30 A.M. A witness, Elizabeth Long, sees Chapman talking to a man outside 29 Hanbury Street. She hears the man ask "Will you?" to which Chapman replies "Yes." Shortly after this sighting, another witness, Albert

Cadosch of 27 Hanbury Street, hears voices in the neighboring yard. He hears a woman say "No!" and then the sound of something falling against the fence that separates No. 27 from No. 29.

4: c. 5:55 A.M. Annie Chapman's body is discovered by John Davis, who lived on the third floor of No. 29.

5: 6:30 A.M. The police pathologist, Dr. George Bagster Philips, arrives on the scene and makes record of Chapman's injuries. In his postmortem report, he considered that the injuries were of such extent, and were executed with such skill, that they probably took no less than 15 minutes to perform.

with which she had met her death. Her throat had been slashed open with two cuts so deep they reached down to her vertebrae, and there were numerous deep slashes across her abdomen.

If this murder had been a once-only occurrence, it is unlikely that it would have been remembered by history. Yet a week later another body appeared. This time the victim was Annie Chapman, a woman with a hard life behind her who had also turned to prostitution. Her body was discovered on September 8, sprawled in the backyard of 29 Hanbury Street, Spitalfields (see "Timeline of a Murder"). The manner of killing was again similar, with deep cuts to the throat and abdomen, but this time the murderer spent a little more time over the mutilations. The following is from the autopsy performed at the time:

"The abdomen had been entirely laid open: the intestines, severed from their mesenteric attachments, had been lifted out of the body and placed on the shoulder of the corpse; whilst from the pelvis, the uterus and its appendages with the upper portion of the vagina and the posterior two thirds of the bladder, had been entirely removed. No trace of these parts could be found and the incisions were cleanly cut, avoiding the rectum, and dividing the vagina low enough to avoid injury to the cervix uteri. Obviously the work was that of an expert—of one, at least, who had such knowledge of anatomical or pathological examinations as to be enabled to secure the pelvic organs with one sweep

of the knife, which must therefore must have at least 5 or 6 inches in length, probably more. The appearance of the cuts confirmed him in the opinion that the instrument, like the one which divided the neck, had been of a very sharp character. The mode in which the knife had been used seemed to indicate great anatomical knowledge."

One of the most chilling elements of the post-mortem report was a suggestion that the horrific attack had been committed by someone with medical knowledge, suggesting that the killer was a man of learning. Now London society, and the police, were giving the murders their full attention.

THE RIPPER

The notoriety of the "Whitechapel Killer," to give him one of his appellations, was further elevated by a letter sent to the Central News Office shortly after the Chapman murder. Opening with the salutation "Dear Boss," the writer first mocked the police efforts to find him, then stated his future intentions with disturbing clarity (the original spelling and grammatical errors are here preserved):

"I am down on whores and I shant quit ripping them till I do get buckled. Grand work the last job was. I gave the lady no time to squeal. How can they catch me now. I love my work and want to start again. You will soon hear of me with my funny little games. I saved some of the proper red stuff in

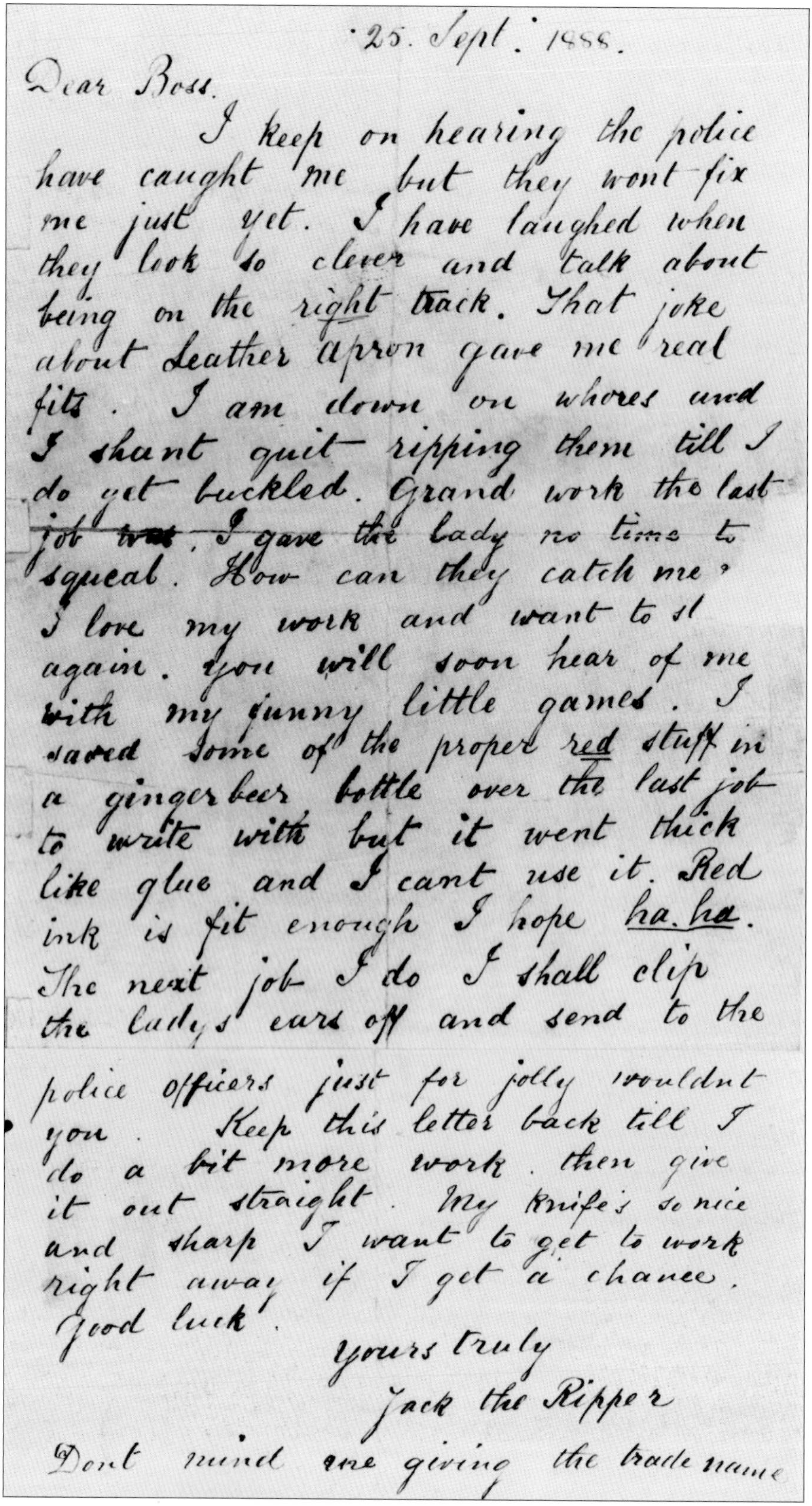

·25. Sept· 1888.

Dear Boss.

      I keep on hearing the police have caught me but they wont fix me just yet. I have laughed when they look so clever and talk about being on the right track. That joke about Leather apron gave me real fits. I am down on whores and I shant quit ripping them till I do get buckled. Grand work the last job was. I gave the lady no time to squeal. How can they catch me now. I love my work and want to st again. You will soon hear of me with my funny little games. I saved some of the proper red stuff in a ginger beer bottle over the last job to write with but it went thick like glue and I cant use it. Red ink is fit enough I hope ha. ha. The next job I do I shall clip the ladys ears off and send to the police officers just for jolly wouldnt you. Keep this letter back till I do a bit more work. then give it out straight. My knifes so nice and sharp I want to get to work right away if I get a chance. Good luck.

        Yours truly

        Jack the Ripper

Dont mind me giving the trade name

a ginger beer bottle over the last job to write with but it went thick like glue and I cant use it. Red ink is fit enough I hope ha. ha. The next job I do I shall clip the ladys ears off and send to the police officers just for jolly wouldn't you. Keep this letter back till I do a bit more work, then give it out straight. My knife's so nice and sharp I want to get to work right away if I get a chance. Good Luck. Yours truly
  Jack the Ripper
  Dont mind me giving the trade name"

◀ A confessional letter from Jack the Ripper written in red ink and delivered to the Central News Office, dated September 25, 1888.

Whether this letter came from the hand of the killer has been debated ever since. The writing style indicates someone literate but not educated, although the writer may well have crunched his own spelling and grammar deliberately to cover his tracks. Yet regardless of its status, the "Jack the Ripper" name stuck.

Soon, however, the letter appeared to be authenticated by another body, that of Elizabeth Stride. Her corpse was discovered at around 1 A.M. on September 30, 1888, in Dutfield's Yard off Berner Street in Whitechapel. The man who came across her body appears to have arrived on the scene just moments after the fatal attack—blood

Timeline of a Murderer—Jack the Ripper's Five Canonical Victims

DATE	VICTIM	AGE	DETAILS
August 31, 1888	Mary Ann Nichols	43	Last seen at the corner of Osborn Street and Whitechapel Road, at 2:30 A.M.; found dead an hour later in Buck's Row, Whitechapel; the small amount of blood at the scene (her throat was slit) suggested that she had been killed elsewhere.
September 8, 1888	Annie Chapman	c. 46	Heavily mutilated body (see "Timeline of a Murder") found in the backyard of 29 Hanbury Street, Spitalfields.
September 30, 1888	Elizabeth Stride	44	Body discovered lying in Dutfield's Yard, off Berner Street, Whitechapel; when discovered by the steward of a nearby club, the body was still pumping blood from the slashed neck, indicating a recent, and interrupted, attack.
September 30, 1888	Catherine Eddowes	45	The second of the Ripper killings on September 30 (although some contend that the Stride killing was not a Ripper murder); her heavily mutilated body was found in Mitre Square, Houndsditch; parts of her body were later sent to George Lusk of the Whitechapel Vigilance Committee.
November 9, 1888	Mary Jane Kelly	c. 25	Murdered in her own lodgings, the killer inflicting extreme mutilations; body was discovered at 10:45 A.M.; neighbors reported the cry of "Murder!" at approximately 4 A.M.

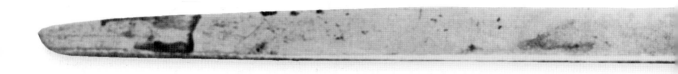

▲ A knife believed to be used by Jack the Ripper. Some of the mutilations on the Ripper's victims exhibited such precision that he has been credited with knowledge of surgery, or at least butchery.

was still pumping out of the woman's slit throat—suggesting that the absence of additional mutilations was simply because the killer was interrupted. (Some researchers claim that Stride was not killed by the Ripper, although most historians still place her in the "Canonical Five" Ripper murders.)

If the Ripper was the murderer, however, he wasn't finished for the evening. Less than an hour after the discovery of Stride's body, another corpse was found, this time in Mitre Square, Houndsditch. This time there was no doubt as to who was responsible. The body of Catherine Eddowes was mutilated in the extreme, with her throat and abdomen slashed and the left kidney, an ear and most of her reproductive system removed. In chalk on the wall above the body, the killer had scrawled "The Juwes are not the men who will be blamed for nothing." The Police Commissioner at the time, Sir Charles Warren, had the message removed before photographs were taken in case it inspired attacks on local Jews.

The Eddowes murder was followed by more letters, ostensibly from the Ripper. A letter sent to the Central News Office, and again signed "Jack the Ripper," stated "I was not codding dear old Boss when I gave you the tip, you'll hear about Saucy Jacky's work tomorrow double event this time number one squealed a bit couldn't finish straight off. ha not the time to get ears for police. thanks for keeping last letter back till I got to work again." Two weeks later, the chairman of the Whitechapel Vigilance Committee (a volunteer force that patrolled the area in the hope of preventing the

Ripper murders, or catching the killer), George Lusk, received a package that contained half a preserved kidney, the accompanying letter reading as follows:

> "From hell.
> Mr Lusk,
> Sor
> I send you half the Kidne I took from one woman and prasarved it for you tother piece I fried and ate it was very nise. I may send you the bloody knif that took it out if you only wate a whil longer
> signed
> Catch me when you can Mishter Lusk"

The opening address "From hell" provided an extra chill to the investigation, and the police found themselves under intense pressure to make an arrest. Yet the case of Jack the Ripper was about to reach its climax.

ATROCITY
The final victim of the "Canonical Five" was Mary Jane Kelly, a c. 25-year-old prostitute known for her attractive appearance. She was murdered on 8–9 November, her body discovered in her lodgings in Miller's Court, lying on her bed, when her landlord came around to collect the rent. The extent of the mutilations was difficult to comprehend. All the flesh of her abdomen and thighs had been stripped off, and the entire abdominal contents removed, the various organs and viscera strewn around the room as if in some obscene act of decoration. Both breasts were cut away. Her face was slashed beyond recognition. Death came from a slashed throat.

Kelly's murder brings to an end, possibly, the murders of Jack the Ripper. The gruesome series of killings simply stopped, although some claimed

(both at the time and since) that five other later murders in Whitechapel could be attributed to the Ripper. Whatever the case, no one was ever arrested for the murders, although there was no shortage of suspects. To date, historians and Ripper specialists have produced a list of no fewer than 31 suspects. They even include Prince Albert Victor, Queen Victoria's grandson, one theory being that the prostitutes were murdered on government orders to cover up Albert's fathering an illegitimate Roman Catholic child. The fact remains that we simply do not know who the Ripper was, despite Herculean efforts by historians and authors to nail the issue once and for all. The mystery surrounding the killer has only served to deepen the fascination with his ghastly crimes.

▶ In recent times historians and researchers have put forward various identities for Jack the Ripper, including Sir William Gull, a prominent society physician and the governor of Guy's Hospital in London.

DAVID BERKOWITZ

In November 1975, 21-year-old David Berkowitz wrote a particularly troubled letter to his father, a letter that revealed a mind in psychotic disorder:

"The world is getting dark now. I can feel it more and more. The people, they are developing a hatred for me. You would not believe how much some people hate me. Many of them want to kill me. I do not even know these people, but still they hate me. Most of them are young. I walk down the street and they spit and kick at me. The girls call me ugly and they bother me the most. The guys just laugh. Anyhow, things will soon change for the better."

Paranoia and a deep antipathy toward women ooze from this letter. Unfortunately for the citizens of New York, such sentiments were soon to be expressed in a long reign of serial murder.

◄ Taking no chances, police officers surround David Berkowitz outside Brooklyn's 84th Precinct after his arrest on August 10, 1977.

Timeline of a Murder

1: It's 1:10 A.M. on July 29, 1976. *Donna Lauria* and her friend *Jodi Valenti* are sitting in a car outside Donna's parents' apartment, talking about their night out at a local disco.

2: Mike and Rose Lauria, Donna's parents, return from their own night out. Mike suggests that Donna walks the family dog before they call it a night. As he goes to get the dog, he notes a yellow car parked close to the apartment. Berkowitz is inside.

3: Donna climbs out of her car, but now notices Berkowitz walking toward her from across the street, carrying a paper bag.

4: As Berkowitz draws close, he pulls a .44 handgun from the bag and fires three shots at both girls. The first shot hits Donna in the chest, killing her instantly, while Jodi is wounded in the thigh.

5: Berkowitz returns quickly to his vehicle and drives away from the scene.

THE JOURNEY TO MURDER

David Berkowitz was born on June 1, 1953. Rejected by his birth mother, he was adopted by Nathan and Pearl Berkowitz, a quiet couple who kept themselves to themselves in the local neighborhood. Pearl's death from pancreatic cancer in 1967 destabilized a boy who was already showing antisocial tendencies—he was known for being something of a bully. Following a poor performance at school, and further unsettled by his father's remarriage in 1971, Berkowitz joined the U.S. Army. His time in the army left two unfortunate legacies. First, he learned how to shoot, and second, he caught a venereal disease from a Korean prostitute, an experience that seems to have left him with a poor opinion of young women in general.

Having left the army in 1974 (his service record was poor, with several disciplinary infractions), Berkowitz went to live in New York, although as the letter quoted above indicates, being back in the city of his birth did not seem to improve his mental health. While in New York he tracked down his birth mother, Betty Falco, but the happy reunion steadily mutated into disappointment. By now Berkowitz's psychosis had reached an explosive stage.

On Christmas Eve 1975, Berkowitz's mind finally snapped. He armed himself with a hunting knife and drove out onto the streets of New York. During the night he attacked and stabbed two women, although both fortunately survived the assaults. He would not attack again for another six months, but in July 1976 he upped the ante by

going out on the hunt again, but this time armed with a powerful .44 Bulldog handgun. At 1 A.M. on the morning of July 29 he came across two women, Donna Lauria and Jody Valenti, sitting in a car outside a bar in the Bronx. Berkowitz simply walked up to the couple and fired at them straight through the windshield, killing Lauria and wounding Valenti.

PATTERN OF PSYCHOSIS

The shooting of Lauria and Valenti laid the foundation for Berkowitz's modus operandi as a serial killer. The following October he struck again. Just like last time he shot a young couple—this time Carl Denaro and Rosemary Keenan—as they sat in a car, although on this occasion both escaped the shooting without fatalities. On November 27, Berkowitz then shot two females sitting outside a house in Queens. Again, both survived the attack, but one of the victims was paralyzed for life by a spinal injury.

Up to this point, New York's public and law enforcement community had not fully engaged with the fact that they now had a serial killer stalking their streets. Now things changed. Ballistics evidence and the manner of the shootings quickly suggested a serial killer, a fact also picked up by the media. Berkowitz then fully confirmed the suspicions with several more killings. On January 30, 1977, 26-year-old Christine Freund was shot while kissing her boyfriend goodnight in his car, and died shortly after. On March 8, one Virginia Voskerichian was shot and killed—the bullet went straight through her mouth—while she was walking home from college. The following April, Berkowitz claimed two more kills, when he shot a young couple dead as they embraced in their car. Yet now came the turning point.

SON OF SAM

At the scene of the last killings, Berkowitz left a letter addressed to Captain Joseph Borelli of the NYPD. The letter did not make for pleasant reading:

"Dear Captain Joseph Borelli, I am deeply hurt by your calling me a woman-hater. I am not. But I am a monster. I am the 'Son of Sam'. I am a little brat. When father Sam gets drunk he gets mean. He beats his family. Sometimes he ties me up to the back of the house. Other times he locks me in the garage. Sam loves to drink blood. 'Go out and kill,' commands father Sam."

More letters followed, the recipients including journalists as well as the police. Soon the whole of New York was abuzz with the hunt for the "Son of Sam." As time would reveal, "Sam" was actually a reference to Berkowitz's neighbor, Sam Carr, whom Berkowitz believed was some form of demon. Dark commands were passed to Berkowitz through Carr's black labrador retriever dog, which at one point Berkowitz actually shot and injured. Unfortunately, it appeared Berkowitz still believed he had more work to do.

In the summer of 1977, Berkowitz shot four more people in two incidents. In the first shooting

▼ Berkowitz's 1970 Ford Galaxie, in which he was arrested in 1977. Police discovered a .44-caliber Bulldog revolver in the car, and matched it to the weapon used in numerous killings.

▲ Westchester County Deputy Sheriff Craig Glassman, who lived near Berkowitz, shows two threatening letters he received. The letters had a similar style of handwriting to those written by the "Son of Sam."

the young couple escaped with minor injuries, but the second shooting resulted in one young woman dead and her boyfriend blinded. Yet from this last shooting came a solid lead for the police.

A witness near the scene of the shooting reported a car speeding away with a parking ticket on its windshield. Police checked both the parking tickets issued that day and cross-referenced them to the description of the vehicle. The information pointed to a vehicle registered by one David Berkowitz of 35 Pine Street, Yonkers. Further details about Berkowitz provided by Sam Carr led police to be confident that they had their man.

The police quickly swooped on Berkowitz's address. They spotted his car, in which the police found a duffel bag holding ammunition and a rifle on the back seat, plus a letter written in the handwriting and style of the Son of Sam. They put the car under observation, and eventually Berkowitz emerged from his apartment block and climbed into the vehicle. The police rushed in and made their arrest—a fact that seemed to amuse Berkowitz.

JUDGED TO BE SANE

The subsequent trial of David Berkowitz rested largely upon evaluations of his mental health—he quickly confessed to the shootings, so responsibility was not in question. Most of the evidence seemed to point to Berkowitz being a sufferer of paranoid schizophrenia. His apartment, for example, was scrawled with messages such as "I kill for my master." Yet other psychiatrists believed that the apparent madness was a pretence, and pushed that he be found sane as well as guilty. This viewpoint prevailed, and on June 12, 1978 he was sentenced to 365 years in prison for six murders. He is in prison to this day.

Timeline of a Murderer—Berkowitz's Shootings

DATE	VICTIM	AGE	DETAILS
July 29, 1976	Donna Lauria	18	Both Lauria and Valenti are shot outside Donna's home in
	Jody Valenti	19	Pelham Bay. Lauria is killed and Valenti injured.
October 23, 1976	Rosemary Keenan	18	Rosemary Keenan and her boyfriend Carl Denaro are shot in
	Carl Denaro	25	Forest Hills Gardens, Queens. Both are injured in the attack.
October 26, 1976	Donna DeMasi	16	Donna DeMasi and Joanne Lomino are shot while chatting
	Joanne Lomino	18	outside Lomino's home. Both are wounded; Joanne is paralyzed.
January 30, 1977	Christine Freund	26	Christine Freund and John Diel are shot in their car outside a
	John Diel	30	movie theater in Queens. Diel suffers superficial injuries, but Freund dies later of her wounds.
March 8, 1977	Virginia Voskerichian	19	Shot as she walks home from Columbia University. She is killed at the scene by a head shot.
April 17, 1977	Alexander Esau	20	Alexander Esau and Valentina Suriani are both shot and
	Valentina Suriani	18	killed at close quarters, the shooting occurring only a few blocks from the Voskerichian shooting.

ROBERT HANSEN

Robert Hansen was a damaged child who grew up into a lethally dangerous adult. What makes his life as a serial killer so distinctive was the method by which he dispatched many of his victims— transporting them into the Alaskan wilderness and then hunting them down like animals.

Born on February 15, 1939, Robert Christian Hansen had the type of childhood that seemed designed to crush his spirit. Living in the shadow of an authoritarian father (at one point his parents tried to force the left-handed boy to be right-handed), as a teenager he suffered from a stammer, terrible acne, bullying, and academic failure. Areas where he did excel, however, were in outdoor and sporting activities, particularly hunting and fishing.

He graduated from high school in 1957, the same year that he joined the Army Reserves, adding

◄ The vast, desolate landscape of Alaska provided a killer's playground for someone like Robert Hansen. He often released his live victims into the wilderness, to hunt them with a rifle or knife.

Timeline of a Murderer—Fates of 11 Identified Victims of Robert Hansen

DATE	VICTIM	DETAILS
Autumn 1979	"Eklutna Annie"	A still-unidentified prostitute stabbed to death in woodland off the Eklutna Road, having earlier got into Hansen's camper van.
1980	Joanne Messina	Hanson took her out for dinner, then later shot and killed her (and her dog) off the Seward Highway, as she became anxious at her apparent abduction.
June 28, 1980	Roxanne Easlund	Went missing after meeting Hansen for a date on Northern Lights Boulevard.
September 6, 1980	Lisa Futrell	An exotic dancer whose body was found in a gravel pit to the north of Anchorage.
November 17, 1981	Sherry Morrow	(see "Timeline of a Murder").
Late November 1981	Andrea Altiery	Hansen abducted Altiery, and forced her at pistol-point to give him oral sex. Afterward she went for his pistol, at which point he shot her dead and dumped her body in the nearby river.
May 26, 1982	Sue Luna	Went missing after meeting Hansen at Alice's 210 Cafe. Her body was found two years later near the Knix River Bridge.
August 1982	Tami Pederson	Murdered after falling for Hansen's promises of a lucrative photo shoot; her body was buried near the grave of Sherry Morrow.
March 25, 1983	Teresa Watson	Murdered around Scenic Lake, and her body left on the frozen ground for animals to eat.
April 1983	DeLynn Frey	Her body wasn't discovered for 16 months after her disappearance.
April 25, 1983	Paula Golding	Dancer at the Great Alaska Bush Company; body found five months later around the Knix River.

Timeline of a Murder

1: November 17, 1981. Exotic dancer *Sherry Morrow* heads out to Alice's 210 Cafe in Anchorage, Alaska. She tells a friend that she is meeting a photographer who has offered her $300 for allowing him to take erotic photos.

2: Having met Hansen, Morrow climbs into his Subaru truck. Once inside the vehicle, Hansen gets violent. He handcuffs and blindfolds her and pushes her onto the vehicle's floor. She lies there while he drives out to a place on the Knix River. There he drags her out of the truck.

3: Distressed at her imprisonment, Morrow resists Hansen's physical attempts to control her. For a time he simply sits

back against a tree, watching her struggle, cradling the .223 Mini-14 rifle that he has now retrieved from the trunk of the vehicle.

4: At one point, Morrow runs up to Hansen, screaming and kicking. He aims the rifle at her and shoots her through the head. He later stated "I just pointed the Mini-14 up toward her and pulled the trigger."

5: Hansen digs a shallow grave in the riverbed and drops Morrow's body into it. He covers her with a thin layer of dirt, and throws the spent cartridge casing from the rifle into the grave.

to his already extensive knowledge of weapons handling. Three years later, by which time he was working in a bakery, he also acquired a wife.

Yet while stabilizing influences seemed to be present in Robert Hansen's life, beneath the surface there was much darkness churning away. He frequented prostitutes on a regular basis, and evidently harbored a deep-seated grudge against his old school by setting fire to it on December 7, 1960. He received three years in prison for the offence, although he served only 20 months, and as a result his wife divorced him.

In 1963 Hansen remarried, and four years later the couple moved to Anchorage, Alaska. His new home suited Hansen down to the ground, offering almost unlimited opportunities for hunting in the state's vast wilderness. He also proved to be extremely good at hunting—some of his kills were entered in world record books. Public respect did not amount

▶ Robert Hansen was a much-respected hunter, an expert in tracking and shooting large game. Here he displays the horns of one of his kills, a mouflon, some of which were entered in international record books.

to private reform, however. He was arrested and convicted of stealing a chainsaw in 1977, and a bakery business he opened in January 1981 was funded entirely on the basis of a fraudulent insurance settlement, in which he claimed that his home had been robbed of valuable hunting trophies. The bakery did well nonetheless, and using the profits he bought his own private airplane (aircraft were and remain a common means of private transportation in Alaska), a Piper Super Cub. The fact that he had never actually acquired a pilot's license seemed unimportant. Being the father of two children by his second marriage, it seemed that in many ways Robert Hansen was at least attempting to present a normal life.

HUNTER

Normality was actually the last thing going on in Robert Hansen's life. From around the autumn of 1979, but possibly earlier, he developed a secret life that consisted of predation, abduction, rape, torture, and murder. Anchorage around this time still had something of a Wild West feel about it, and tough men and many prostitutes frequented the town.

Hansen regularly went into the Tenderloin district and picked up prostitutes and erotic dancers, often with the promise of good money for allowing him to do a photo shoot. If they bought his story, he would take them in his aircraft or truck out to the Knix River Valley, a wild area 25 miles (40km) from Anchorage and known for its extensive big-game hunting.

There Hansen owned a remote hunting cabin, and once the girls were there they were essentially his prisoners. Some simply submitted to his violent sexual desires, and were later flown back to Anchorage. Yet others were brutally raped and then had to face a terrifying final ordeal. Turning them loose into a wilderness with which most were not familiar, Hansen gave the girls a short head start, then tracked them down with his hunting rifles as if he was pursuing a bear, goat, or deer. Invariably, he caught up with them and shot them, burying their bodies in a environment so expansive that he was confident they would never be discovered.

In total, Robert Hansen would murder 17 women and girls in this or a similar manner, although the vagueness of his memories and the fact that many of the bodies were never recovered make the exact details uncertain.

GETTING NOTICED

By mid-1983, Alaskan police officers were aware that something bad was happening to the prostitutes and dancing girls of Anchorage. In 1980 the badly decomposed body of a (still) unidentified woman was discovered near the Eklutna Road near the Eklutna Lake, evidence showing that she had been murdered by a gunshot. Soon afterward, the body of another woman, Joanne Messina, was discovered dumped in a gravel pit in the same area. With the discovery of dancer Sherry Morrow's body in September 1982, the police realized that one man was likely to be perpetrating all the killings. Officers staked out local bars and clubs, covertly gathering information from the girls and their own observations on anyone who appeared suspicious, or who had strange or violent sexual tendencies.

An initial break came on June 13, 1983. A local prostitute known as Kitty Larson had been picked up by Hansen, taken back to his house in Anchorage, handcuffed, and violently sexually assaulted (at one point he had even shoved a

hammer into her vagina). She managed to escape, handcuffs still dangling from one wrist, just before he could force her onto his plane. A passing trucker rescued her and took her to the police, where she told them all about Hansen.

Here was a chance to break the cycle of killing, but it slipped through the police's fingers. Hansen simply denied the girl's story, producing alibis in the form of some local friends. Faced simply with her word against his, the police had to let Hansen go. Yet less than three months later, the discovery of another body, that of 17-year-old Paula Golding, led police to look once again at Robert Hansen. They pulled in his friends for questioning, and his previously solid alibis for the Kitty Larson case fell apart under more aggressive questioning. The officers acquired a search warrant for Hansen's house, and on October 27, 1983 they discovered a secret compartment in the attic rafters that contained several firearms, including a .223 Mini-14 rifle whose shell casings would match those found at the scene of the wilderness murders. More incriminating still, the box also contained jewelry and ID cards that belonged to some of the victims.

BARGAINING

Hansen realized that the game was up, and he pleaded guilty to four of the known murders. Here the Anchorage District Attorney, Victor Krumm, then offered him a deal—in return for a complete confession of all his crimes (evidence indicated that there were many more than four murders), he would only be charged with the four cases currently brought against him. Furthermore, he would be sent to regular federal prison, rather than a maximum security institution.

Hansen agreed to the conditions and subsequently confessed to a total of 17 murders. He also led police officers to various grave sites around the Alaskan wilderness, from which they recovered 11 bodies. Many of the bodies were discovered after Hanson received a sentence of 461 years plus life on February 27, 1984.

▼ A Piper Super Cub aircraft, of the type used by Robert Hansen to take potential victims out to his hunting lodge in the Alaskan wilderness. Many individuals in Alaska own aircraft, so being invited into his plane wouldn't usually arouse suspicion among the women he picked up.

RANDY KRAFT

To this day we still do not know how many men Randy Steven Kraft has killed. His conviction for 16 murders alone makes him a significant figure in the history of U.S. serial killers, yet his actual total could reach as high as 67. At the time of writing, he waits on death row for the final delivery of his sentence.

R andy Stephen Kraft was born on March 19, 1945 in Long Beach, California. Apart from being particularly accident-prone, Kraft seems to have had a relatively normal and conventional childhood. His family having moved to Westminster, Orange County, in 1948, Kraft developed into an active and intelligent adolescent, known for holding the conservative views typical of the area in which he was living. He graduated from Westminster High School in 1963, his academic performance putting him in the top 10 of his class, and he went on to

◀ The beaches of California were the perfect cruising ground for Randy Kraft. The 1970s were also a time in which thousands of people drifted in and out of California, making murder investigations complicated.

Timeline of a Murder

1: December 31, 1975. Twenty-two-year-old *Mark Hall* is enjoying a New Year's Eve party in San Juan Capistrano. At some point during the evening, he meets Randy Kraft, and leaves the party with him. Hall had been drinking alcohol and his body was later found to contain traces of Diazepam and Valium.

2: Kraft and Hall travel out to the Cleveland National Forest, heading to the east end of Santiago Canyon in the Saddleback Mountains. This location is about 30 miles (48km) south of San Juan Capistrano.

3: What occurred is largely based upon forensic evidence derived from Hall's body. It appeared that Hall had been stripped and tied to a tree sapling. He was then sodomized and tortured horribly. Parts of his body were burnt with a cigarette lighter or cut with a sharp knife. His genitals were removed, and stuffed into his rectum. It is also likely that Kraft was forcibly administered more alcohol, and pushed earth and leaves into both Hall's mouth and anus. He died at the scene of his wounds and strangulation.

4: Hall's body was discovered on January 3, 1976. A bottle was found at the scene which had Kraft's fingerprints on it. This was later used by prosecutors to connect Kraft with the murder.

study economics at the prestigious Claremont Men's College.

So far, so good. It was between the ages of 18 and 20, however, that Kraft's personality seemed to enter a confusing stage. At first he appeared resolutely conservative in his political and social outlook, joining the Reserve Officers' Training Corps (ROTC), and throwing himself into the presidential campaign of right-wing candidate Barry Goldwater. He was also vocal in his support for U.S. military involvement in Vietnam. Yet in 1964 he changed sides, becoming left wing in political orientation, backed by growing long hair. Furthermore, it was around this time that his sexuality went through significant transformation. By the time he was 18 he had realized that he was homosexual, and there were many campus rumors about his predilection for bondage. He began frequenting gay bars, and in 1966 he was also arrested after having offered himself for sex to an undercover vice officer—he was released with a caution.

In 1968 Kraft joined the U.S. Air Force. He was only in the service for a year before he was discharged on "medical grounds" in 1969, incidentally the same year that he told his family he was gay. His revelation alienated him from his conservative parents, and from now on Randy Kraft seemed to go off the rails.

FIRST VICTIMS

From the early 1970s, Kraft's lifestyle was focused on a combination of frequent sex with various men and a hefty intake of drugs, particularly speed. In March 1970, an incident also revealed another side of his personality. He managed to lure a 13-year-old runaway boy called Joseph Alwyn Fancher back to his home, where he plied the boy with drink and drugs then raped him violently. Fancher managed to escape the incident with his life, and reported it to the police. The story hung together, but a subsequent police search of Kraft's apartment—which turned up both drugs and highly explicit photographs—was conducted without a warrant, and so the police were unable to proceed with the case.

Having got away with violent assault, it now appears that Kraft moved on to murder. His first victim was possibly Wayne Joseph Dukette, found dead and decomposing on October 5, 1971 along the Oretaga Highway. There is some uncertainty, however, about whether responsibility for this death lay with Kraft. Many sources put his first official victim, therefore, as 20-year-old Edward Daniel Moore, a U.S. Marine. (Kraft had a particular fondness for Marines, there being two major Marine Corps bases in California.) His corpse, found by the side of the 405 Freeway at Seal Beach on December 26, 1972, was a sobering sight for homicide detectives. He had been beaten and strangled to death, and one of his socks had been pushed up his anus. His genitals showed clear signs of being bitten.

Three more bodies soon built up the undeniable impression that there was a serial killer stalking the highways and beaches of southern California. Moreover, it was apparent that the manner of killing was becoming increasingly depraved. The first body, of an unknown male, was discovered on February 6, 1973 beside a freeway in Wilmington, Los Angeles, again with one of his socks pushed up his anus. The next body (another unknown male), however, had its genitals removed, leading to the possibility that the man simply bled to death from the mutilation, although there were also signs of strangulation. Another victim found shortly afterward had his head thrown on to Long Beach,

▼ Randy Kraft listens in a courtroom in Santa Ana, California, as the jury recommends that he should die in the gas chamber. His death sentence was confirmed by the Supreme Court in 2000.

while his torso, one leg and both arms were found in the next county on Sunset Beach. Clearly, California's gay men were being hunted by someone with monstrous appetites.

CATCHING A MONSTER

It is ironic that even as Randy Kraft was slaughtering men on a regular basis throughout California, he was actually in a semisteady relationship with one Jeff Seelig. In 1982 he even went for counseling to try to help their relationship improve. He also had a serious relationship with Jeff Graves, a former classmate. Furthermore, Kraft found steady, respectable employment—in 1975, he began working as a computer programer for Pacific Computing Systems. Balanced against this normality, however, were crimes of almost

unbelievable brutality. Some serial killers focus on delivering an efficient killing without using consciously designed tortures. Randy Kraft was not one of them. Typical injuries inflicted upon his victims include castration, a variety of objects inserted into the penis or the anus (of the latter, some were as large as substantial tree branches several feet long), decapitations, burns from a cigarette lighter and bites to genitals and nipples.

In January 1975, a multicounty police task force was formed to pursue the serial killer. Because of the nature of the crimes, police and FBI psychologists were brought in to create profiles of the potential killer. Bodies were turning up every few weeks or months, and the pressure was on to find the man responsible. Kraft did in fact briefly pass through police hands in June 1975, after he was arrested for lewd behavior in Cherry Park. He spent five days in jail before being released, after which he resumed killing where he left off.

Despite the number of bodies, the police were still struggling to get close to the killer. Kraft was not, in fact, the only serial killer operating in California during these years. In 1977, for example, Patrick Kearney was arrested and confessed to the murder of 28 young men. Such killers made investigating Kraft's murders that much more complicated, and his killing spree would continue for another five years. In fact, it could be argued that the sheer volume of his murders made the job of the police that much harder,

Timeline of a Murderer—Known Victims of Randy Kraft

NB: Many of the dates of death are provided by the California Death Index, which essentially records when the death was registered. The actual murder date could vary slightly.

DATE	VICTIM	AGE	DETAILS
September 24, 1971	Wayne Joseph Dukette	30	Possibly Kraft's oldest victim.
December 24, 1972	Edward Daniel Moore	20	U.S. Marine serving at Camp Pendleton; body dumped near the 7th Street exit of the 605 Freeway; one sock was inserted into his anus.
February 1973	unidentified male	18–20	Found on the Terminal Island Freeway on February 6, 1973; strangled to death.
April 1973	unidentified male	?	Found in Huntington Beach.
April 1973	unidentified male	?	Body was refrigerated prior to being dumped.
c. July 30, 1973	Ronnie Gene Wiebe	?	Last seen at the Sportsman Bar in Los Alamitos.
December 23, 1973	Vicente Cruz Mestas	23	Discovered by hikers in the San Bernardino foothills.
June 2, 1974	Malcolm Eugene Little	20	Truck driver from Selma, Alabama, visiting his brother in Long Beach; murdered after being picked up while hitchhiking.
June 22, 1974	Roger E. Dickerson	20	U.S. Marine; disappeared after accepting a lift to Los Angeles.
c. August 2, 1974	Thomas Paxton Lee	25	Waiter in San Pedro; body dumped in a Long Beach oil field.
August 12, 1974	Gary Wayne Cordova	23	Body found on highway in Orange County.
Late November 1974	James Reeves	19	Last seen alive leaving a gay church in Costa Mesa after Thanksgiving.

by producing a vast multiplicity of false leads and investigative dead ends.

The ultimate break came on May 14, 1983, when officers of the California Highway Patrol pulled over someone driving erratically on the San Diego freeway. The driver was Randy Kraft and having stepped out of the car and performed badly during a sobriety test, he was arrested for drunk driving. Yet a far more serious offence related to the dead man, 25-year-old Marine Terry Gambrel, who lay in the passenger seat of the car. He had been strangled, but also had near-lethal amounts of drink and drugs in his system. Now treating the suspect with utmost caution, the police searched his car further and found a pack of Polaroid photos

showing dozens of apparently lifeless men, and also a sheet of paper containing what appeared to be a coded list of men murdered by Kraft. A later search of Kraft's home produced a mass of further forensic evidence, including more photographs of murder victims plus personal effects of many of the dead.

After a lengthy trial, Randy Kraft was convicted of 16 counts of murder on November 29, 1989, and he was sentenced to death. In a curious act of futile bravado, in 1992 Kraft attempted to launch a massive lawsuit against an author who painted his character in a less than favorable light. Not surprisingly, the lawsuit was rejected, and in August 2000 his death sentence was again confirmed by the Supreme Court.

DATE	VICTIM	AGE	DETAILS
c. January 3, 1975	John W. Leras	17	Body found on Sunset Beach on January 3, 1975.
17 January 17, 1975	Craig Victor Jonaitis	21	Body found at Long Beach Motel on Pacific Coast Highway.
c. March 26, 1975	Keith Daven Crotwell	19	Victim's head discovered on May 8 off Long Beach, and other remains found the following October.
January 3, 1976	Mark H. Hall	22	(see "Timeline of a Murder").
c. April 1978	Scott Michael Hughes	18	Murdered in Orange County.
June 10/11 1978	Roland Gerald Young	23	Thrown from a moving vehicle when dead; genitals severed and stabbed to death.
June 19, 1978	Richard Allen Keith	20	Body found in Laguna Hills in June 1978; strangled to death.
July 6, 1978	Keith Arthur Klingbeil	23	Body found on the northbound lanes of Interstate 5, near Mission Viejo, in Orange County.
November 18, 1978	Michael Joseph Inderbieten	21	Burned with a cigarette lighter and his genitals severed.
June 16, 1979	Donnie Harold Crisel	20	
September 3, 1980	Robert Wyatt Loggins	19	Photos of Loggins' body were found in Kraft's home.
January 27, 1983	Eric Herbert Church	21	Semen found on body matched Kraft's blood type.
February 12, 1983	Geoffrey Alan Nelson	18	Body discovered in Garden Grove.
May 14, 1983	Terry Lee Gambrel	25	Body discovered in Kraft's car when he was pulled over for driving while intoxicated.

THE YORKSHIRE RIPPER

For six years, Peter William Sutcliffe stalked the streets of Yorkshire in northern England. Between 1975 and 1980, he murdered a total of 13 women, usually followed a characteristically awful *modus operandi*—typically battering them to death or unconsciousness with a ball-peen hammer, then finishing the job with a knife or sharpened Phillips screwdriver. Once it became clear to police, by 1977, that the killings were the work of the same man, there followed one of the biggest murder investigations in British history.

Peter Sutcliffe was born on June 2, 1946 in Bingley, West Yorkshire. His childhood was the typically troubled one seen in many serial killers. Quiet, bullied and with few friends, Sutcliffe clung mainly to his mother for affection, and left school when he was 15 to pursue

◄ Police keep guard on Peter Sutcliffe's home in Bradford just after his arrest in Sheffield on January 2, 1981. Sutcliffe had been stopped in a car with a prostitute, his arrest likely preventing another murder.

Timeline of a Murderer—Known Victims of Peter Sutcliffe

DATE	VICTIM	AGE	DETAILS
October 30, 1975	Wilma McCann	28	Murdered in Prince Phillip Playing Fields, Leeds, after getting into Sutcliffe's car following a night out.
January 20, 1976	Emily Jackson	42	Bludgeoned with a hammer, then stabbed 52 times with a screwdriver. Her body was found in Manor Street, Sheepscar, Leeds.
February 5, 1977	Irene Richardson	28	Murdered in Roundhay Park, Leeds, on the site of an earlier (non-fatal) Sutcliffe attack.
April 23, 1977	Patricia Atkinson	32	Murdered in her own home at Flat 3, 9 Oak Avenue, Bradford.
June 26, 1977	Jayne MacDonald	16	Killed on Reginald Street, Leeds; Sutcliffe's first non-prostitute victim.
October 1, 1977	Jean Jordan	20	Killed in the allotments next to Southern Cemetery, Manchester, indicating that Sutcliffe was expanding his territory.
January 21, 1978	Yvonne Pearson	21	Left under a discarded sofa in an empty lot off Arthington Street, Bradford.
January 31, 1978	Helen Rytka	18	Stabbed and beaten to death and left in a timber yard on Great Northern Street, Huddersfield.
May 16, 1978	Vera Millward	40	Murdered in a remote corner of the grounds of Manchester Royal Infirmary.
April 4, 1979	Josephine Whitaker	19	Murdered in Savile Park, Halifax. Whitaker and the remainder of Sutcliffe's victims had nothing to do with prostitution.
September 2, 1979	Barbara Leach	20	Final-year psychology student murdered in Bradford.
August 20, 1980	Marguerite Walls	47	Murdered in Farsley, Leeds. Sutcliffe used a rope to strangle Walls, rather than his usual hammer and sharpened screwdriver, aiming to throw police off his trail.
November 17, 1980	Jacqueline Hill	20	Sutcliffe's last victim, found on an empty lot off Alma Road, Headingley, Leeds.

a string of dead-end jobs, including that of grave-digger. Nevertheless, Sutcliffe seemed to achieve a degree of normality. His personality grew enough for him to meet and date Czech immigrant Sonia Szurma; they moved into her parents' house when they married in 1974. Yet Sonia's husband was living a double life. Sutcliffe regularly used prostitutes to fulfil his extra-marital lusts, a habit facilitated by the Heavy Goods Vehicle (HGV) license he acquired in June 1975, allowing him to

Timeline of a Murder

1: Saturday June 25, 1977. Sixteen-year-old store clerk *Jayne MacDonald* has been out for the evening around Leeds with friends. She misses the last bus home, but spends a few hours in the company of a man she had met during the evening. They go their separate ways at 1:30 A.M. on June 26 near St. James Hospital.

2: 1:30 A.M. Jayne is unable to call a taxi, so decides to walk home. The route home takes her through the area where Peter Sutcliffe often goes "hunting."

3: 2 A.M. Peter Sutcliffe spots Jayne while driving down Chapletown Road. He parks his car and gets out, arming himself with a hammer and a kitchen knife. He later claimed that he believed she was a prostitute.

4: On Reginald Street, Sutcliffe approaches Jayne from behind and makes his attack. He strikes the back of her head with the hammer, then drags her unconscious form into a nearby playground. There her kills her, the final wound count including three hammer blows to the head and about 20 stab wounds. A broken bottle was also found stuck in her chest, although Sutcliffe later claimed that this probably occurred as he dragged her across the ground.

5: Sutcliffe leaves Jayne's body in the playground, after having attempted to wipe his knife clean on her clothing.

spend time away from home indulging his sexual needs and, soon, darker pathologies.

FIRST MURDERS

At his trial in 1981, Sutcliffe told the court, with psychotic sincerity, that in his early 20s the voice of God had commanded him to go out and murder prostitutes. These auditory hallucinations continued to bubble away for the next nine years, until they finally burst out on July 4, 1975 in the town of Keighley. Local woman Anna Patricia Rogulskyj was subject to a violent hammer and knife attack outside her home; only the intervention of her neighbor saved her from certain death. (Note that Sutcliffe had in fact attacked a prostitute in 1969, striking her with a stone swung in a sock, although this first incident doesn't seem to have been an attempted murder.)

Sutcliffe's first attack had failed. He tried again a month later. This time his victim was 46-year-old Olivia Smelt, whose life was saved, once again, by the timely arrival of a third party. Proving he had scant regard for age, he next attacked a 16-year-old girl in Silsden, who also survived. Despite the fact that all the victims were prostitutes from similar areas, and the manner of attack was the same, police had yet to suspect that there was a new potential serial killer on their patch.

The first three major attacks in Sutcliffe's dreadful career as a murderer had not resulted in fatalities, mainly on account of the opportune intervention of others. This situation was about to change. On October 30, 1975, 28-year-old mother of four Wilma McCann was subjected to Sutcliffe's undistracted violence—she was battered to death a short distance from her home. Police now began to suspect the truth, that a sick individual was preying on the prostitutes of Yorkshire. Their suspicions were grotesquely confirmed on January 20, 1976, when the smashed body of Emily Jackson, a 42-year-old prostitute, was discovered in Manor Street, Sheepscar, Leeds. The following June, prostitute Marcella Claxton became another of Sutcliffe's victims to survive following a hammer attack, but seven months later a prostitute from Leeds, Irene Richardson, was murdered in typical Sutcliffe fashion. He was getting into the swing of killing.

MANHUNT

During the first two years of Sutcliffe's killings, the police painfully accrued additional information with each addition to the body count. They had a semen sample; wellington boot imprints on the thigh of Emily Jackson; tire tracks near the body of Irene Richardson. A fourth murder in April 1977, that of Bradford prostitute Patricia Atkinson, provided more clues but no single, definitive lead. The nature of the hunt for the killer changed dramatically on June 26, 1977, however. On that day Sutcliffe battered to death 16-year-old Jayne MacDonald. The previous victims had been prostitutes, a career that always dampened sympathy from the public and moderated interest from the media. MacDonald, however, was simply a store clerk.

Now that the threat appeared to have widened to all women of northeast England, the public interest exploded. The killer was dubbed the "Yorkshire Ripper," a name that regularly graced the news headlines as Sutcliffe added more victims. Police investigators were inundated with information and suspicions from the public, some of value, but most doing little more than scatter

police attention and resources. The whirlwind of publicity surrounding his crimes did not stop Sutcliffe from committing more crimes—far from it. He attacked again on July 9, his victim (Maureen

Long) surviving the attack to add to the forensic picture being steadily built up by police. His next victim, Jean Jordan from Manchester, died on October 1 from Sutcliffe's horrible assault, with an extra macabre twist. Sutcliffe had initially paid Jordan for her services with a brand new, and highly traceable, £5 banknote from his wage package. Later realizing that this item was still in her handbag, Sutcliffe went back to find it. Failing to do so, he subjected Jordan's corpse to further horrific mutilation.

The subsequent police search of the murder area did indeed discover both the handbag and the note, the latter eventually leading them to interview personnel at Sutcliffe's place of work. Sutcliffe himself appeared before the police investigators. This incredible chance to stop future murders slipped through the law's fingers. Sutcliffe, totally calm and plausible, told the officers he was not in the murder area on the night in question. Backed up by the false testimony of his wife Sonia, Sutcliffe slipped through the net.

INTENSIFICATION

From October 1977 to May 1978, Sutcliffe's murderous activities seemed to hit a peak. During this period he murdered four more women and seriously injured another. The survivor provided the first detailed description of the Ripper, correctly describing the dark curly hair and beard that would later be seen in the widely circulated photo of Sutcliffe during and after his trial. From May 1978, however, his killings seemed to stop. Sutcliffe's mother was terminally ill, and died on November 8, 1978, and her illness and his grief seemed to temporarily divert his attentions. Furthermore, there were tragic problems with the police investigation. Letters, and eventually an audio recording, from Sunderland claimed to be from the Yorkshire Ripper himself. Forensic evidence seemed to authenticate these leads, so much so that even though Peter Sutcliffe was brought in for interview on several occasions by the police, he was released on account of his profile not matching that of the

◀ A photograph of Peter Sutcliffe, sitting in the cab of his truck at the Bradford engineering firm T.W. Clark, where he worked as a driver in the 1970s. Itinerant jobs suited his predatory activities.

Sunderland suspect. Known to the police as "Wearside Jack," the origin of the voice and the letters was actually that of fantasist John Humble, a former security guard. In 2006, Humble was convicted on the basis of DNA evidence taken from one of the letters and was imprisoned for eight years. Yet the damage he did during the Ripper investigation was critical, diverting officers and man-hours to investigating his fantasies rather than discovering the actual killer.

After 11 quiet months, meanwhile, Sutcliffe decided to return to killing. A Bradford student (not a prostitute) named Barbara Leach was beaten and stabbed to death on September 2, 1979, and 11 months later one Marguerite Walls was throttled to death with a rope, Sutcliffe changing his killing method to confuse police. Walls was also not a prostitute but a civil servant. It appeared that Sutcliffe's mental distortions were now directed against the whole female population, not just prostitutes, with a concomitant increase in public fears.

In total, Sutcliffe would carry out three more attacks before justice caught up with him. Two, in September and early November 1980, were non-fatal. On November 17, however, Sutcliffe stabbed to death student Jacqueline Hill. By now the police had finally dismissed the "Wearside Jack" evidence, but the net would finally close around Sutcliffe largely by accident.

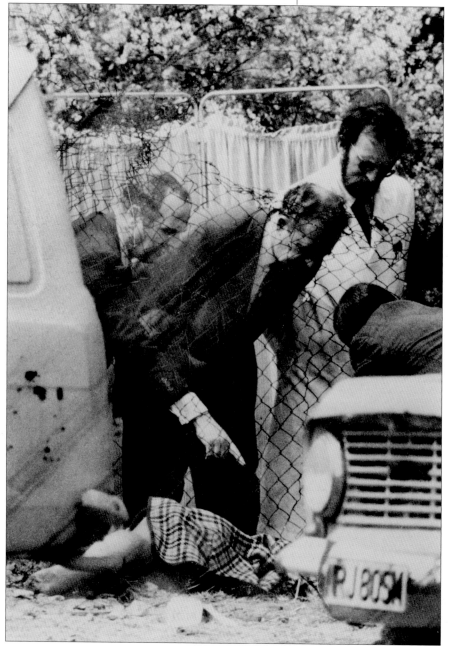

◄ Detectives inspect the body of another victim of Peter Sutcliffe. The murders took place over five years and challenged the police with several false leads and lines of enquiry.

ARREST AND TRIAL

The big break came on January 2, 1981. Sutcliffe was arrested in a car with a prostitute, and it was discovered that his car license plates were false. He also gave his name as Peter Williams, a name that he later retracted in the police station. Once they had his real name, police unearthed Sutcliffe's connections with the Ripper investigations, and also noted that he bore a striking resemblance to the best descriptions of the attacker. A blood test confirmed that he had the same blood group (B) as the blood left by the attacker on his victims. Then came the clincher.

An officer remembered that when first arrested, Sutcliffe had requested that he be allowed to urinate, which he did behind a nearby storage tank at the scene. An officer traveled back out to the scene, and behind the storage tank found Sutcliffe's discarded hammer and knife. When confronted with all the evidence. Sutcliffe admitted to being the Yorkshire Ripper. He did so without emotion, listing all his crimes over a 26-hour interview. The Ripper's reign of terror was at an end.

Despite legal representations that Sutcliffe was suffering from paranoid schizophrenia, he stood conventional trial on May 5, 1981. The jury deemed him both sane and guilty, however, and on May 22 he was sent to prison for life. Sutcliffe remains in prison to this day. His name, like those of Myra Hindley and Ian Brady, remains synonymous with pure, home-grown evil among the British people.

▼ Press and public gather outside the Old Bailey courthouse in London, during the trial of Peter Sutcliffe in 1981. Sutcliffe was eventually found guilty of 13 counts of murder, and sentenced to life imprisonment.

BELTWAY SNIPER ATTACKS

At 5:20 P.M. on October 2, 2002, Ann Chapman was preparing for the end of the day at the hobby retailers in Aspen Hill, Maryland, at which she worked as a cashier. With no warning, the window of the shop suddenly cracked and she felt the wind of a high-velocity .223 rifle bullet crack past her head, so close that it touched her hair. She had just survived the first attempted killing by the individual who would become known as the Beltway Sniper (so called because he seemed to use the Washington Beltway road system to move between attacks), a person who for the next three weeks would terrorize the states of Washington D.C., Maryland, and Virginia. By October 24, 10 people were dead and three were seriously injured.

◀ The funeral of 35-year-old bus driver Conrad Johnson, shot dead by John Allen Muhammad on October 22, 2002. He was the last victim of the "Beltway Sniper" attacks.

Timeline of a Murder

1: October 3, 2002. 8:46 A.M. *Sarah Ramos*, a 34-year-old Salvadorean immigrant of Silver Springs, Maryland, sits on a bench outside the Leisure World Shopping Center in Aspen Hill. Ramos works several jobs, and is waiting for a bus to come to take her to another place of work.

2: *John Allen Muhammad* and *John Lee Malvo* are parked nearby in their blue Chevrolet Caprice. They have already shot two people dead in the last hour, one at 7:41 A.M. and the next at 8:12. They spot Ramos sat on the bench, reading to pass the time.

3: Muhammed moves into the rear of the car, lying flat on the specially designed luggage compartment. In the rear of the trunk, he has already drilled two holes—one for

the muzzle of the weapon, and the other for the telescopic sight of the gun. He now takes aim at Ramos.

4: 8:47 A.M. Muhammed fires a single shot. Witnesses at the scene recall hearing a crack, then seeing Ramos slump forward, with blood pouring from her head. The .223 bullet from Muhammed's Bushmaster rifle destroys Ramos' brain and skull, killing her instantly.

5: Muhammed and Malvo, having taken a young, promising and innocent life, pull away from the scene. They will kill two more people that day alone. Initial 911 calls at the scene report that the women has shot herself. Only when police investigators arrive do they realize that she has been shot by a third party.

LETHAL ACCURACY

Within 45 minutes of the shooting at Aspen Hill, the Beltway Sniper took his second shot. This time his aim was perfect—a single bullet killed 55-year-old James Martin as he walked across the parking lot of a Glenmont supermarket. These incidents in themselves warranted a major police investigation, but nothing prepared the local police for what would occur the following day, Thursday October 3. Between 7:41 A.M. and 9:15 P.M., the faceless sniper shot dead another five people. What was apparent was that the selection of victims had a distinctly random quality about it. They included 39-year-old landscaper James

▶ John Allen Muhammad arrives in the Prince William Circuit Court in Manassas. He described the murders he committed as part of a "Jihad" (holy war'), but the real motivation seems unclear.

Buchanan, 34-year-old housecleaner Sarah Ramos, and 72-year-old father of five Pascal Charlot. All had been killed in open, public locations within reach of major roadways.

By the end of the day, it was not only state and Federal law enforcement agencies that were bursting into action, but also a startled urban media. Panic rippled through the public, stirred even further by the shooting of a 43-year-old mother of two, Caroline Seawell, as she loaded up her minivan with goods outside a mall in Spotsylvania County, Virginia. She survived, but for the citizens using and living around the Washington Beltway, casual activities such as filling the car at a gas station or using a supermarket now seemed fraught with risk.

The main figurehead of the police investigation into the murders was the police chief of Montgomery County, Charles Moose. The Montgomery County police, however, provided the command center for a particularly wide investigation that involved agencies such as the Virginia Department of Transportation, the Bureau of Alcohol, Tobacco, and Firearms (BATF) and the FBI. All pooled their forensic and investigatory resources in an attempt to find the killer before he struck again.

TAROT CARD KILLER

Unfortunately, for many days to come the Beltway Sniper seem to have the advantage. At 8:09 A.M. on

▲ Police search a park across from where Conrad Johnson was fatally shot. Johnson, a Montgomery County bus driver, had been standing in the doorway of his bus when hit by the bullet.

Monday October 7, shortly after Charles Moose had cautiously reassured the public that there was no reason to keep children off school, the sniper put a bullet through 13-year-old Iran Brown outside the Benjamin Tasker Middle School in Bowie, Maryland. Incredibly the boy survived, but for the police it was apparent that not only was the sniper feeding off the media coverage, but he was also a potential child killer. There was another alarming development—the Death card from a pack of Tarot Cards was found at the scene of the shooting inscribed with the words "Call me God." In addition to the title Beltway Sniper, the shooter was now also labeled the "Tarot Card Killer." Radio and TV broadcasts were now filled with experts, real and professed, who offered profiles of the killer and suggestions as to how the police could track him down. Yet despite hurling huge law enforcement resources at the case, the sniper seemed to remain elusive.

FINDING A KILLER

Between the Iran Brown shooting and October 22, five more people were shot dead by the sniper, mostly in parking lots or gas stations around Virginia and Maryland. The killer was also becoming bolder, more taunting. He started to leave messages and letters around the scenes of the shootings, boasting to the police about his impunity while also making blackmail demands for millions of dollars and

threatening that "Your children are not safe, anywhere, at any time." Yet the sniper's confidence would actually be his undoing. In a mocking phone call to Chief Moose's office, the sniper mentioned his involvement in an armed robbery in Montgomery, Alabama, in September 2002, during which a liquor store clerk was shot dead. The FBI pulled details of the crime, and obtained fingerprints from a handgun magazine dropped near the scene of the crime. The FBI ran the fingerprints through their national database, and found that they belonged to 17-year-old John Lee Malvo, a known associate of 41-year-old ex-soldier John Allen Muhammad.

Vehicle license checks revealed that Muhammed owned a blue Chevrolet Caprice that had been checked during random traffic stops around the areas of the shootings over the past few weeks. (For many days during the investigation, the police had been looking for a white box van believed to be associated with the shootings, although investigations into this

Timeline of a Murderer—the Beltway Shootings

DATE	VICTIM	AGE	DETAILS
October 2, 2002	None		At 5:20 P.M. a shot is fired through a window of a Michaels Craft Store in Aspen Hill, Maryland. No one is injured.
October 2, 2002	James Martin	55	At 6:30 P.M. Martin is shot and killed in the parking lot of a Shoppers Food Warehouse grocery store, Glenmont.
October 3, 2002	James L. Buchanan	39	At 7:41 A.M. landscaper Buchanan is shot dead near Rockville, Maryland, while mowing the grass at the Fitzgerald Auto Mall.
October 3, 2002	Premkumar Walekar	54	At 8:12 A.M. part-time taxi driver is killed in Aspen Hill in Montgomery County, while filling his car at a Mobil gas station.
October 3, 2002	Sarah Ramos	34	At 8:47 A.M. Ramos is shot and killed at the Leisure World Shopping Center in Aspen Hill, while seated on a bench, reading a book.
October 3, 2002	Lori Ann Lewis-Rivera	25	At 9:58 A.M. shot and killed while vacuuming her Dodge Caravan at a Shell station in Kensington, Maryland.
October 3, 2002	Pascal Charlot	72	At 9:15 P.M. Charlot is shot while walking on Georgia Avenue at Kalmia Road, in Washington DC. He dies of his injuries shortly afterward.

vehicle proved to be wasted time.) On October 24, around 3 A.M., the blue Caprice was spotted in a parking lot in Frederick, Maryland. Within minutes, police and FBI tactical units surrounded the vehicle and apprehended Malvo and Muhammad, who both gave themselves up with surprising compliance. Discovered in a bag in the car was Muhammad's Bushmaster XM-15 .223 rifle, which forensics later linked to 11 of the 14 shootings. Further investigations revealed that the Caprice had been modified so that Muhammed could lay across the floor of the trunk and shoot through a small aperture drilled into the trunk itself, a modification that explained the inability of witnesses to provide sightings of the shooter.

PROFILING

John Allen Muhammad and John Lee Malvo were a curious pair. Muhammed was the sniper—he had served in the U.S. Army for nine years, during which time he saw active service in the first Gulf War (1990–1) and became classified as an expert in M16 rifle marksmanship. (The Bushmaster XM-15 is a civilian/law enforcement version of the military M16.) Malvo seemed to have simply acted as his compliant sidekick. Muhammad was actually born John Williams, but later changed his surname to reflect a conversion to Islam in the 1980s. His life up to the murders was a litany of emotional, marital and commercial failures. If we were to spot a final catalyst for killing spree, it may have been when his (second) ex-wife won full custody of their three children, with a restraining order placed upon Muhammad. Many people go through tough lives without resorting to serial murder. During the trial in 2003, the court found both men guilty, sentencing Malvo to life imprisonment without parole and Muhammad to death. Despite his appeals, Muhammad was executed by lethal injection on November 10, 2009.

DATE	VICTIM	AGE	DETAILS
October 4, 2002	Caroline Seawell	43	At 2:30 P.M. Seawell is shot and wounded in the parking lot of a Michaels Craft Store at Spotsylvania Mall in Spotsylvania County, Virginia, while loading purchases into her minivan.
October 7, 2002	Iran Brown	13	At 8:09 A.M. Brown is shot and injured outside the Benjamin Tasker Middle School in Bowie, Maryland.
October 9, 2002	Dean Harold Meyers	53	At 8:18 P.M. Meyers is shot dead while pumping fuel at a Sunoco gas station on Sudley Road in Prince William County, Virginia.
October 11, 2002	Kenneth Bridges	53	At 9:30 A.M. Bridges is shot dead while pumping fuel at an Exxon station off Interstate 95 in Spotsylvania County, Virginia.
October 14, 2002	Linda Franklin	47	At 9:15 P.M. Franklin, an FBI intelligence analyst, is shot dead at a Home Depot in Fairfax County, Virginia.
October 19, 2002	Jeffrey Hopper	37	At 8 P.M. Hopper is shot and injured in a parking lot near the Ponderosa Steakhouse in Ashland, Virginia.
October 22, 2002	Conrad Johnson	?	At 5:56 A.M. Bus driver Johnson is shot dead on the steps of his bus in Aspen Hill, Maryland.

JANE TOPPAN

The story of Jane Toppan, like that of Harold Shipman and other medical murderers, has a special resonance with our fears. When we are sick we are at our most vulnerable, and the thought that a doctor or nurse might seek to harm rather than heal is particularly chilling. Such is the case with Toppan, who like an angel of death murdered an unknown number of sick people—at least 31—between 1887 and 1901, while ostensibly caring for them.

Jane Toppan was born in 1854 in Lowell, Massachusetts. Her birth name was Honora (Nora) Kelley, and she was raised initially by her father, Peter Kelley, after her mother died when she was very young. In time, however, Peter Kelley descended into insanity and alcoholism. Nora and her elder sister went into the care of the Boston Female Asylum and then, in 1859, into the hands of foster parents, Ann and Abner Toppan.

◀ The home of Oramel Brigham, the husband of Jane Toppan's late foster sister. Jane herself sits on the stoop, and she would go on to murder Oramel's sister and other members of his family.

Timeline of a Murder

1: Late June 1901. *Mary "Mattie" Davis* journeys over to the house where Jane Toppan is lodging. She is Jane's personal friend, and visits to settle some financial arrangements concerning a vacation home with Toppan's landlords, Melvin and Eliza Beedle. Incidentally, Toppan has already there been poisoning the Beedles, but only enough to give them the appearance of gastrointestinal illness.

2: Once Mattie arrives, Toppan gives Mattie a drink of poisoned Hunyadi water (a mildly laxative mineral water). By the evening Mattie is feeling extremely sick, and so Toppan begins to administer morphine for the pain.

3: Toppan controls subsequent doses of morphine over the next seven days. She alternates Mattie's condition between consciousness and unconsciousness, making sure that the woman does not stay lucid for very long.

4: A doctor visits the apparently dying woman. Even though the doctor in question has experience in investigating poisoning murders, he is only familiar with killings using arsenic, and so fails to spot the signs of morphine poisoning.

5: Mattie Davis finally dies on July 5. Jane then moves in with her family and sets about killing three other members of the household.

The relationship between Jane Toppan and her foster parents—Ann changed the girl's name soon after adoption—was not a great one. The Toppans had another foster daughter, Elizabeth, who was given preferential love and affection, and the relationship between Ann and Jane was abrasive. Jane herself eventually became something of a recluse, a situation exacerbated by a failed engagement in her early adulthood, the distress of which resulted in two suicide attempts.

Jane finally broke free of her old life at the age of 26, when she left home and went to study nursing in Cambridge, Massachusetts. It was during her time at medical school that some unwholesome aspects of her character began to emerge. Fellow students noted how she seemed to have something of a obsession with visiting the mortuary and observing postmortems. Gradually, this obsession contorted into a determination to commit murder on a regular basis.

ANGEL OF DEATH

The beginning of Jane Toppan's life as a serial killer seems to date around 1885, while still at the Cambridge Hospital. She began testing out mixtures of morphine and atropine on vulnerable patients, injecting them with the substances and gaining a thrill from seeing them slip close to death. She would fake results on their medical charts in order to cover her tracks. Soon she was taking the next step, selecting and murdering patients on the basis of whim. Toppan murdered an unknown number of

people between 1885 and 1890, not only in Cambridge Hospital but also in the Massachusetts General Hospital. Much later in life, when she delivered a confession of her crimes, she testified that watching the individuals die gave her something of a sexual thrill. As they slipped from this world to the next, she would often cuddle up in bed with them, holding their juddering and weakening bodies as they died.

Although the other doctors and nurses were unable to pin anything concrete on Toppan, they were aware that her ministrations didn't seem to do her patients any good. Combined with evidence that she had misused hospital opiates, these concerns resulted in her dismissal from hospital service in 1891. Undeterred, Toppan resolved to go to work as a private nurse, where her activities would come under far less scrutiny.

Between 1891 and 1899, Toppan killed a variety of people, including her landlord, her foster sister, and an old friend (see Timeline). For in her self-employed capacity, often traveling around the homes of New England's wealthy patrons, she could kill with increasing regularity. Yet it was the attention that she paid to one particular family that would leave her exposed to suspicion. In July 1901, Toppan attended the funeral of one of her victims, Mrs. Mattie Davis. (Mattie had actually died during a personal visit to Toppan, whom she classed as a friend.) Toppan's graveside devotion was so convincing that the family of the deceased asked her to stay on as their private nurse, as at that time sickness was running through the family. It was a truly fatal request. The sicknesses were probably caused, or at least promoted, by Toppan herself—as well as killing people during her long and twisted career, Toppan also had a habit of prolonging the illnesses of people for whom she enjoyed working. The first to fall was Annie Gordon, Mattie's married eldest daughter. Her health took a considerable downturn following her mother's funeral, and on July 29 Toppan gave her a substantial injection in order to "ease her sufferings." Predictably enough, by the time a doctor actually arrived at Annie's bedside, the unfortunate woman was dead. Despite two of the Davis family being killed in less than a month, and the common denominator being Jane Toppan, still the family did not suspect any foul play. Capitalizing on the Davis' trusting nature, Toppan then went on to murder Mattie's grieving husband, Alden Davis, blaming his sudden death on a stroke. At this point, the surviving daughter, Mary Gibbs, was growing less than comfortable with Jane Toppan's presence. Her mariner husband was away on a sea voyage at this time, so she requested that a cousin, Beulah, come to stay with her to watch what was happening. The extra pair of eyes proved insufficient,

however, and by the middle of August Mary Gibbs was also dead.

Having murdered virtually the entire Davis family, Toppan now moved back to her hometown, where she turned her predatory instincts upon her own foster family. In a bizarre plan, she tried to build a relationship with her dead foster sister's husband, Oramel Brigham, by murdering his sister,

▶ A portrait of Jane Toppan, painted when she was just 17. By this age Jane had already experienced familial rejection and death, beginning to warp her personality. In seven years she would start to kill.

◄ One of Jane Toppan's victims, Mary E. Gibbs. Mary was one of four members of the same household killed by Toppan in July and August 1901, having been taken into the house as a family nurse. Their deaths gave police solid leads in their investigations.

returned from sea to find his family drastically reduced. He was immediately suspicious of Toppan, especially when he heard from Beulah that she had refused permission for an autopsy of Mary's body on "religious grounds."

Captain Gibbs acted decisively. He informed the police of his fears and his wife's body was exhumed for medical examination. As he feared, the postmortem quickly revealed that his wife had been murdered, with morphine being the method of killing.

On October 29, 1901, Toppan was finally arrested by police in Amherst, New Hampshire, her arrest coming just in time to save the family for whom she was working. At first Toppan protested her innocence, stating that,

Mrs. Edna Bannister, and poisoning Oramel, whom she thought would be impressed by her tender ability to bring him back to health. She was wrong, however, and the obviously intuitive husband rejected her advances.

CONFESSION

While Toppan was destroying members of her own family, Captain Gibbs, Mary's husband, had

"I have a clear conscience. I wouldn't kill a chicken, and if there is any justice in Massachusetts they will let me go." Yet as the police began to exhume more and more of her victims, she began to change her tune. By 1902 she had confessed to the murders of 11 people: the four members of the Davis family and seven others. Her confessions give a troubling insight into her state of mind:

"Yes, I killed all of them. I might have killed George Nichols and his sister [members of the family with whom she was working at the time of her arrest] that night if for detective hadn't taken me away. I fooled them all—I fooled the stupid doctors and the ignorant relatives; I have been fooling them for years and years ... I read [the prosecutor's] statements about me poisoning people with arsenic. Ridiculous, if I had used arsenic my patients would have died hard deaths. I could not bear to see them suffer. When I kill anyone they go to sleep and never wake up. I use morphia and atropia, the latter to hide the effects of the former. It took days sometimes to kill them."

The insanity of Jane Toppan was argued by several psychiatrists. They pointed not only to the nature of the murders themselves, but also to the history of insanity that ran in her natural family—not only her biological father, but also one of her sisters had been committed to a lunatic asylum.

Jane Toppan was finally convicted of 11 murders on June 23, 1902 in Barnstable County Courthouse, a court finding her not guilty by reason of insanity. She was committed to Taunton Insane Hospital, but with her conviction came further admissions of murder. She told her lawyer that she had killed more than 31 people, with the possibility that the number of homicides might actually be as many as 70. Because of poor recordkeeping on the part of the Massachusetts medical authorities of the day, it is impossible to discover all her victims, nor when they actually died.

In an ironic postscript to this story, Jane Toppan spent the rest of her days in the asylum, often claiming that the staff of the institution were trying to poison her. She finally died in 1938, aged 84.

Timeline of a Murderer—Known Victims of Jane Toppan

DATE	DETAILS
1887	Toppan begins killing patients while working at Boston's Cambridge Hospital, then Massachusetts General Hospital. It is probable that she killed dozens of patients during this period of employment.
1895	Toppan poisons her landlord Israel Dunham, complaining that he is a "fussy" character. After the murder, she moves in with his wife, Lovey.
1897	Toppan murders Lovey Dunham.
1899	In August, Toppan fatally poisons her foster sister, Elizabeth Brigham. Mary McNear, an old lady recommended into Toppan's care, is murdered.
1900	Murders an old friend, Myra Connors, in order to take over her position as a dining matron at a theological school.
1901	Toppan murders four members of the Davis household—Mattie Davis, Annie Gordon, Alden Davis, and Mary Gibbs—over a period of five weeks in July–August. Having left the Davis house, she returns to Lowell and murders Edna Bannister.

DOROTHEA PUENTE

Although the world of serial killers is largely the preserve of men, it is not exclusively so. Just such an exception to the general rule is Dorothea Puente. In 1993 this white-haired old lady went on trial for the murder of nine people, although she was implicated in many more disappearances. How she got to this stage is a tale of lust, greed, and failure.

Dorothea Puente was actually born Dorothea Helen Gray on January 9, 1929 in Redlands, California. Her home life was fractured from the word go. One of six children, her father died of tuberculosis in 1937 and less than a year later her mother was killed in a vehicle accident. From this point on she went through various homes, being passed among members of the family around southern California.

◄ Dorothea Montalvo Puente talks with her attorneys in 1990 in court at Sacramento, California. Her appearance was almost the exact opposite of how people imagined a serial killer.

Timeline of a Murder

NB: The following is based on circumstantial evidence.

1: February 1987. *Leona Carpenter*, 78 years old, moves into 1426 F Street, having recently been discharged from hospital. She goes into the care of *Dorothea Puente*, who takes payment for her residence.

2: Carpenter spends several weeks lying on the sofa, convalescing from her time in hospital. Around this time, however, she suddenly goes missing.

3: Likely evidence suggests that Puente gave Carpenter a lethal dose of Fluazepam/Dalmane, a prescription sleeping pill that can have a lethal effects if given in excessive doses, especially among alcoholics, drug addicts, and the elderly.

4: Carpenter's body is buried near the back fence in Puente's garden. In November 1989, Detective John Caberra found what at first sight appear to be a tree stump in Puente's back garden. He pulled on the stump, and so unearthed a human thigh bone that opened up the investigation into Puente's murders.

Unsurprisingly, she began to show an unsettled character. At the age of only 16, she fled her then foster parents and moved to Olympia in Washington State, where she changed her name to Sheri and worked in a milkshake parlor. She also began to make some extra money through prostitution.

A dominant theme of the life of Dorothea Puente is a tendency for repeated marriage and divorce. Her first husband was 22-year-old soldier Fred McFaul (Dorothea had told him that she was 30 years old). Although they had two daughters together (raised by others), the marriage was not a happy one—McFaul (no saint himself) tired of her constant and outrageous lying and excessive vanity, and subsequently left her. By this time, Dorothea was living back in California.

It was now that Dorothea gained her first experiences of a criminal career. In 1948 she stole some government checks and used them to buy clothes. Caught and convicted of forgery, she went to jail for four years. The brush with the law did not reform Dorothea. In 1952 she married sailor Axel Johansson, and although this marriage was to last 14 years it was a far from stable relationship. Dorothea's frequent infidelities (made easier by Axel's long periods away at sea), which included a spell working in a brothel, plus constant arguments brought the marriage crashing down in 1968. Not one to stay down for long, Dorothea married 21-year-old Jose Puente just a year later, and would be known by his surname for the rest of her life.

For the single year they were together, Dorothea and Jose ran a halfway house, taking in alcoholics and drifters who paid for their keep using social security checks. The business was not a success—it collapsed under $10,000 of debt by the time the marriage failed. Yet it was this "business model" to which Dorothea would return throughout her life, and which would eventually provide her with the opportunity for murder.

SPIRALING DOWN

Despite her previous failed business, Puente's next employment was as the manager of another halfway house in Sacramento. Opportunistic love quickly blossomed, and in 1976 she married one of the residents, Pedro Montalvo, but that marriage also rapidly broke down. Two years later she was once again arrested and convicted of forging checks, stolen from the people staying in her care. Rather than sending her to prison again, the judge instead gave her five years on probation plus a program of psychological counseling. Whatever counseling she received doesn't seem to have worked. In fact, she was about to commit murder.

Puente's first victim was 61-year-old Ruth Munroe, a resident of her boarding house. Munroe also developed something of business partnership with Puente, but what Puente really had in her sights was the $6,000 in cash in Munroe's possession. After only a few weeks of living at 1426 F Street, Munroe was dead, killed by a large overdose of codeine and Tylenol. The subsequent legal investigation wrote off

▶ Police use a digger to explore the garden of Puente's Sacramento home. A total of seven decaying bodies were found in the garden, the victims all killed within a 21-month period.

Munroe's death as suicide, and Puente was duly encouraged. She began drugging elderly residents of the boarding house, robbing them as they lay unconscious or in a stupor. Yet she was becoming sloppy with her pharmaceutical technique—one victim even testified to watching her rob him as he lay there in a nonfatal catatonia.

This time the authorities did act, convicting Puente of robbery and sentencing her to five years in prison, of which she served only three years. Evidently the police did not make any link between these particular crimes and the death of Munroe just months earlier.

INTENSIFICATION

When she was released from the California Institution for Women at Frontera in September 1985, Puente had no intention of going straight. While in prison, she had struck up a correspondence relationship with 77-year-old Everson Gilmouth from Oregon. Incautiously, Gilmouth gave Puente details of his pension arrangements, and believed that he had fallen in love with the younger inmate. When she was released, therefore, Gilmouth met her from prison, gave her access to his bank account and paid for her accommodation at 1426 F Street.

Gilmouth's impetuous nature cost him his life. Shortly after Puente's release from prison, he went missing. In January 1986, his rotted body was discovered in a crude coffin by the side of the Sacramento River, and it would be another three years before he was finally identified. (The coffin was the work of Ismael Florez, a local handyman whom Puente had asked to build her a "wooden box" with the dimensions of a coffin.)

Gilmouth was Puente's second known murder victim, but he would by no means be her last. In clear violation of the terms of her parole, Puente eventually turned 1426 F Street into a boarding house, taking in a collection of residents passed across to her by the Sacramento social services. A simple background check would have revealed just how unsuitable Puente was for looking after elderly and vulnerable people, but the fact that Puente would accept difficult, antisocial residents made her a valued asset to an overstretched government department. With a captive group of residents, Puente was to murder in significant numbers.

Between February 1987 and November 1988, more residents went missing. They included 62-year-old James Gallop, 62-year-old Vera Martin and 52-year-old Alvaro Montoya. Drugged and murdered, these people and others were disposed of around the grounds of the house. Puente then continued to cash their social security checks—she cashed more than 60 checks in the names of dead residents.

It was inevitable that someone would eventually become suspicious about the activities of Puente and 1426 F Street. Ironically, Puente would not be rumbled by the state parole officers, who visited her no fewer than 15 times over two years but were never aware of the fact that she was running a boarding house for the elderly. Yet some of the people who had been killed were naturally missed by their relatives, who became suspicious and reported their disappearance to the authorities. Police investigators went around to 1426 F Street, and while walking around the backyard one of the detectives happened to discover a human leg bone.

MURDER ENQUIRY

What had begun as a missing person investigation now turned into a major murder enquiry. The grounds of the house were dug up, and the police discovered a total of seven bodies in various states of decay. Mutilations indicated that Puente had become quite used to the mechanics of death and disposal—some of the bodies were found to be missing heads and limbs.

Despite her elderly appearance and her gender, Puente was quickly suspect number one. Autopsies of the bodies discovered traces of Fluazepam/ Dalmane, and a cross-check with Puente's criminal record indicated that drugging was her preferred method of murder. Combined with the evidence from the cashed social security checks, the net was now closing in around Dorothea Puente.

Here the police made a blunder. During the second day of digging around her house, Puente— who hadn't been arrested at this point—slipped out to a local hotel, ostensibly to grab a coffee. She fled, taking a bus to Los Angeles, where she adopted the name Donna Johansson. Presenting herself as a grieving widow down on her luck, she even befriended 59-year-old Charles Willgues and, after enquiring into his social security situation, suggested that they move in together. The rightly cautious Willgues resisted the idea, and back at his apartment later that evening his memory of local news stories suddenly triggered his suspicions about the real identity of the lady. Willgues first contacted a local TV station; they in turn got in touch with the police, who swooped and arrested Dorothea Puente.

LIFE IMPRISONMENT

The trial of Dorothea Puente was lengthy and complex, and was made more psychologically confusing for the jury by the grandmotherly appearance Puente adopted for the courtroom (simple long dresses, pearl necklace, glasses, and white, permed hair). The need to gather sufficient evidence meant that the trial did not begin until February 1993, even though she'd been charged with nine counts of murder back in March 1989. Her defense team presented Puente as a sweet and innocent old lady, who hadn't reported the deaths of her residents because she was afraid that she would be sent back to prison for parole violation. Puente showed no signs of emotion throughout the trial, not even when the jury were presented with graphic photographs of the bodies rotting in her garden. Yet the prosecution still had to prove, through circumstantial evidence alone, that this old woman was a serial killer.

The complexities of the case are reflected in the fact that on their first attempt to come to a verdict, the jury was deadlocked. A subsequent attempt, however, found Puente guilty of only three of the murders. This was enough, however, for Dorothea Puente to receive life imprisonment without parole. Today she is still serving out the sentence in Central California Women's Facility, maintaining her innocence but kept well away from the society on which she preyed.

Timeline of a Murderer—Known Victims of Dorothea Puente

DATE	VICTIM	AGE	DETAILS
1982	Ruth F. Munroe	61	Dies of a drug overdose in Puente's house at 1426 F Street.
September 1985	Everson T. Gilmouth	77	Drugged and murdered, his body disposed of by the side of the Sacramento River in a makeshift coffin.
February 1987–November 1988:			
	Dorothy Miller	65	A Native American lady with an alcohol problem. When found her arms were taped across her chest with duct tape.
	Leona Carpenter	78	A hospital discharge resident, whose leg bone marked the beginning of the investigation.
	Vera Faye Martin	65	A resident of 1426 F Street from October 1987.
	Betty Mae Palmer	78	Her body had its head, hands, and lower legs removed.
	James A. Gallop	62	Went to stay at 1426 F Street following medical treatment for both a heart attack and a brain tumor.
	Benjamin Fink	55	A vulnerable alcoholic resident.
	Alvaro Montoya	52	A deeply disturbed schizophrenic, whose body was buried under an apricot tree.

AILEEN WUORNOS

The United States has been no stranger to female serial killers throughout its long history. During the 1990s, however, one Aileen Wuornos was branded by the U.S. media as "the first female serial killer." Historically, the label was inaccurate, but it evokes both the sensation caused by this deeply disturbed and predatory woman, and the disbelief that the "gentler sex" was capable of such systematic murder.

O n February 29, 1956, Aileen Carol Pittman was born in Rochester, Michigan. The leap year date may have seemed auspicious, but the infant's family circumstances were far from promising. Aileen's mother, Diane, was just 17 years old, and her husband of two years, Dale Pittman, left her while she was pregnant with Aileen. (By this time, Diane already had a son named Keith.) A

◀ Aileen Wuornos, here seen on trial in 1992. Wuornos confessed to most of her crimes, but her explanations about why she committed them were often questionable and inconsistent.

paranoid schizophrenic, Dale would end up incarcerated in mental institutions following convictions for child abuse. Although it was a blessing that Aileen would grow up free from his influence, there remains the question of what genetic legacy Dale left his unwanted daughter. (Dale hanged himself in 1969.)

Diane finally had enough of her responsibilities when Aileen was four years old, and abandoned her and her brother. The duty of raising them passed to their Finnish grandparents, Lauri and Britta Wuornos, who lived in Troy, Michigan. The move did not bring the security nor love the children desperately needed in these formative years. Later Aileen alleged that she was sexually abused by her grandfather and beaten regularly by both grandparents. Whatever the reality of these claims, it is true that she grew into a disruptive and aggressive adolescent. She was sexually promiscuous by the time she was 12 years old, and had her first child at the age of 15—it went straight to adoption. Shortly afterward, her grandmother died, and both children became wards of court.

From then on it was downhill fast for the young girl. By the time she was in her late teens, she was working as a prostitute between intermittent dead-end jobs, and getting in regular trouble with the law, not only for prostitution but also on charges such as drunk driving and disorderly conduct. She also appeared to be developing an early love affair with firearms—on one occasion she was arrested and charged for having fired a gun from a moving vehicle—and in her early 20s had also been charged with assault.

As Aileen drifted across America, there were a couple of potential bright spots. In Florida, she met a wealthy 69-year-old yacht club president, Lewis Fell, and struck up an unlikely relationship. They were married in March 1976, but within a few months the marriage was annulled—Fell discovered that Aileen's tendency to fight in bars spilled over into the home, when Aileen beat her aging husband with his own cane. Shortly afterward, Aileen shot herself in the stomach in a botched suicide attempt.

Also in 1976, Aileen inherited $10,000 when Keith died from throat cancer in July. In now characteristic style, she took all the money and blew it within two months on drink, drugs, and a car (which she crashed and destroyed). At this point it was hard to see how the life of Aileen Wuornos could get much lower.

DESCENT

The 1980s marked a new, and appalling, era in the life of Aileen Wuornos. Having squandered an opportunistic marriage and a sudden inheritance, she embraced crime as her principal means of

▼ **The Last Resort Bar in Port Orange, Florida, the scene of Wuornos' arrest for an outstanding warrant (not a murder charge). Only when she was in custody did police begin to connect her with the murders.**

Timeline of a Murder

1: May 19, 1990. *David Spears* of Bradenton, Florida, informs his boss (Spears is a heavy equipment operator) that he is going to be heading up to Orlando, to visit his ex-wife. He sets off that day from his workplace in Sarasota.

2: While traveling through Citrus County, he picks up Aileen Wuornos. It is likely that they had sex, as a used condom was later found near his naked (apart from a baseball cap) body.

3: Having had sex, Wuornos produces the .22 handgun she carried with her. She shoots Spears a total of six times, killing him at the scene.

4: Wuornos dumps Spears' body along Interstate 75 in Citrus County. She has removed the license plate and leaves the doors to the vehicle unlocked.

5: Later, at Ormand Beach, Wuornos pawns a set of machine tools that match the description of those taken from Spears' truck.

▲ The story of Aileen Wuornos even caught the attention of Holywood. Actress Charlize Theron (right) plays Wuornos in the 2003 movie *Monster,* here alongside Christina Ricci.

getting by. She returned to prostitution for income, but also diversified into robbery and fraud. Many of her nonviolent crimes have an almost laughable incompetence, such as holding up a supermarket in 1981 while wearing only a bikini, for which she spent the best part of two years in prison. Once released, she didn't break step—she was arrested numerous times between 1983 and 1986 for charges ranging from grand theft auto to using forged checks.

Through all this murky daily life, however, Wuornos had managed to strike up an unexpected relationship. Having doubtless fostered a generally poor impression of men throughout her life, she met and began a lesbian relationship with 24-year-old Tyria Moore. Wuornos attempted to support them both financially, a commitment that saw her increase her number of sexual clients to up to a dozen a day, with the associated beatings and nonpayments that were part and parcel of her risky trade. To protect herself, she carried around a .22 caliber handgun, a weapon that soon found regular use.

OPPORTUNITY FOR MURDER

On December 1, 1989, Wuornos was picked up by a 51-year-old owner of an electronics repair outlet, Richard Mallory. Buying her services, Mallory drove down to woodland near Daytona Beach. Later, at her trial, Wuornos testified that at the beach Mallory had violently sexually assaulted her, and she killed him in self-defense. Whatever the truth, it appeared that the couple drank a bottle of vodka between them, before Wuornos produced her .22 handgun and shot him four times. Once he was dead, she emptied his wallet and drove home in Mallory's car—his body was found dumped in a junkyard, and the car was later abandoned. Once home, Wuornos actually told Moore what she had done, although in court Moore testified that she did not believe her.

Two points that make the truth about this first killing uncertain are: 1) Mallory actually had a conviction for rape, so Wuornos' rape accusation is not implausible; 2) Wuornos used the self-defense plea in relation to all her subsequent murders, thereby reducing its evidential force. What is beyond doubt, however, is that Mallory was just the first in a long line of murders. Aileen Wuornos had taken the first step to becoming a serial killer.

All of Wuornos' remaining killings—six in total—were performed in 1990, with each following a similar pattern. The next victim was 43-year-old David Spears, who picked her up in his truck in May 1990—the following month his naked corpse was discovered in woodland. He had been shot six times and his truck stolen. Florida law enforcement officers began to suspect they had a serial killer on their hands when they later found the body of 40-year-old Charles Carskaddon, who had also been shot six times and robbed of his money, valuables (including a gun) and his car (dumped the following day).

Timeline of a Murderer—Known Victims of Aileen Wuornos

DATE	VICTIM	AGE	DETAILS
December 1, 1989	Richard Mallory	51	Shot several times near Daytona Beach and his body dumped; the body was found on December 13, 1989.
May 19, 1990	David Spears	43	Shot six times along Highway 19 in Citrus County; body found on June 1, 1990.
May 21–22, 1990	Charles Carskaddon	40	Shot nine times; body found on June 6, 1990, in Pasco County.
June 7–8, 1990	Peter Siems	65	Body never found—connected to Wuornos by palm print on car door handle.
July 30, 1990	Troy Burress	50	Shot twice; body found on August 4, 1990 in a wooded area in Marion County.
September 11, 1990	Charles "Dick" Humphreys	56	Shot six times in the head and torso; body found on September 12, 1990 in Marion County.
November 17, 1990	Walter Gino Antonio	62	Shot four times; body found on November 19, 1990 near a logging road in Dixie County.

Just a few days later, in early June, Wuornos' victim was Christian outreach worker Peter Siems, 65, driving to Arkansas through Florida. By this stage she was typically picking up men by hitchhiking, and Siems was terribly unlucky whom he helped on this occasion. Siems' body was never found, but Wuornos began to make her first serious mistakes, first by hanging on to his car for more than a day. On July 4, she and Moore crashed the car near Orange Springs. They abandoned the vehicle shortly afterward, but from this incident the police were able both to identify Siems' car and gain a description of the two women from eyewitnesses to the accident. The police were now fully awake to the possibility that a woman or women were murdering men in the Florida area.

Between July and November 1990, police discovered three more bodies, all murdered in a now familiar fashion. Troy Burress, 50, a sausage salesman from Ocala, was murdered on July 30, 1990, but his body was not discovered until the following August. Similarly, the body of 56-year-old Charles "Dick" Humphreys, a retired Air Force major and former Chief of Police, was discovered shot six times in Suwanee County in September, although his killing had been much earlier in the year. The final murder was of 62-year-old Walter Jeno Antonio, killed on November 17 and his body discovered the same day. His abandoned car turned up five days later.

THE NET CLOSES

As with so many other serial killers, the arrest of Aileen Wuornos began with an investigation for a far more trivial offence than murder. On January 9, 1991, by which time Moore had left her, police picked up Wuornos on an outstanding firearms violation. Once in custody, they also began connecting her to the murders, confirmed by palm-print evidence from Siems' car and the eyewitness descriptions from the vehicle accident. The police tracked down Moore in Pittston, Pennsylvania. In return for prosecutorial immunity, Moore agreed to help police acquire evidence against Wuornos for the murders; she allowed them to tape phone conversations between her and Wuornos, which provided substantial material in the later court case. Furthermore, on January 16, Wuornos confessed to the murders, but argued that all had been carried out in self-defense against violent customers.

◀ Peter Siems, murdered by Wuornos in June 1990. Siems' body was never found, but Wuornos was connected with his death via her palm-print discovered on his car. Wuornos would, however, go on to murder three more men after Siems between July and November 1990.

▲ Members of the press photograph Father Fred Ruse of Winter Haven, Florida, who holds a banner reading "Choose Life" in protest at the execution of Aileen Wuornos by lethal injection on October 9, 2002.

Wuornos did not go to trial for another year. When she did so, in January 1992, there was a media storm. The relentlessly grim details of her life appealed to the major news networks, and even to Hollywood, which would later go on to make a major movie of her life. Her trial was specifically focused on the murder of Richard Mallory, although she had already made a videotaped confession to the murder of all seven victims. All through the trial, Wuornos protested that she was the victim rather than Mallory, but outlandish and inconsistent accounts of the events and of her own life undermined her credibility as a defendant. (The court also gave special jurisdiction to admit previous crimes and convictions as contextual evidence.) The final nail in the coffin of her testimony was a court appearance by Moore. Ultimately, the jury came back with the expected "guilty" verdict, to which Wuornos screamed "scumbags of America." The sentence was death.

Wuornos moved onto death row, and she began a deranged series of appeals, hiring and firing attorneys. She was tried for the murders of all her other victims apart from Peter Siems, as his body was never discovered. So by early 1993, Wuornos had received a total of six death sentences, from which she could not escape.

EXECUTION

Wuornos would spend nine years on death row, during which time her grip on reality seemed to become ever more tenuous. She gave several interviews during her incarceration, to both the media and professional psychiatrists. These interviews were typified by explosive rants against society and an extremely disturbed demeanor, although all three psychiatrists who were tasked with assessing her mental state deemed her sufficiently self-aware to be executed. During an interview with Nick Broomfield, a British documentary filmmaker, she once again insisted that the murders were self-defense; she claimed she was publicly saying otherwise so she could simply get her harrowing stay on death row over with, and be executed.

On October 9, 2002, Wuornos drank her last cup of coffee—she had refused a last meal—and was led to her execution chamber. There she was killed via lethal injection. Whatever the nature of her crimes, hers was undoubtedly a life critically and horribly wasted from the very earliest years.

THE MOORS MURDERERS

It is hard to overestimate the extent to which Myra Hindley and Ian Brady shocked British society during the late 1960s. The shock came not just from the nature of what they did—murder five children for the purposes of sexual gratification—but also from the fact that one of the people involved was a woman, her acts assaulting the traditional ideas of maternal protective instincts.

Myra Hindley and Ian Brady met in 1961 in Manchester, when Hindley found work as a secretary for the Millwards Merchandising company in Gorton, at which Brady was employed as a bookkeeper. Only 18 years old, and just recently out of a failed engagement, Hindley was much attracted toward Brady's brooding and seemingly exciting character. There was something a little bit

◄ October 22, 1965. Police officers and members of the public scour Saddleworth Moor following the arrest of Myra Hindley and Ian Brady. The body of John Kilbride, 12, was found later that day.

Timeline of a Murder

1: July 12, 1963. In the early evening, 16-year-old *Pauline Reade* is on her way to a dance at the Railway Workers' Social Club in Crumpsall, Manchester. At the same time, Ian Brady and Myra Hindley are patrolling the local streets, looking out for a victim. Hindley is driving a van, and Brady is following a short way behind her on a motorcycle. They have agreed that when he spots a potential victim, Brady will flash his lights and Hindley will stop and attempt to pick her up.

2: Around 8 P.M., on Froxmer Street, Brady spots Pauline Reade and flashes his lights. Hindley pulls over and starts talking to Pauline, the introduction made easier by the fact that Pauline is a friend of Hindley's younger sister. Hindley asks Pauline if she can help her look for an expensive glove she has lost on Saddleworth Moor. Pauline agrees and gets into the van.

3: Up on Saddleworth Moor, Hindley introduces Pauline to Brady, under the pretense that he has also come to look for the glove. According to Hindley, she then left Pauline in Brady's company. After about 30 minutes Brady walks back across the moor alone, and comes to get Hindley.

4: Brady takes Hindley to the location where Pauline is dying from a slit throat. Her clothes are disheveled and clearly indicate a sexual assault. Brady tells Hindley to stay with Pauline while he goes to fetch a spade to bury the body. Note that in Brady's later version of events, Hindley was a active participant in both the sexual assault and the murder.

5: Once Brady returns and buries the dead girl, the couple then lift the motorcycle into the back of the van and drive home. On the way home they pass Pauline's mother and brother in the streets looking for the missing girl.

dangerous about Brady, and certainly his life to date had been colorful. Born in Glasgow on January 2, 1938, Brady was a bright young man, yet one whose personality was unsettled by his upbringing in a broken home. His unmarried mother was forced to give him up when he was four months old, sending him to live with a local couple who already had four children of their own.

As he grew older, Brady slipped into a life of minor crime. After several brushes with the law, in late 1954 he was ordered to move to Manchester as part of his probationary conditions, to live once again with his birth mother. (His mother, Maggie Stewart, had by this time married, and Brady took this stepfather's surname.) Brady was later sentenced to two years (1955–57) in reform school for stealing a large quantity of lead seals. After his release he went through a string of manual jobs, but then seemed to attempt to better himself. Despite his issues, Brady always had something of an academic spark within him. Some of this was expressed in worrying ways—he developed a fascination with Nazi philosophy, and was an avid reader of Hitler's *Mein Kampf* alongside works such as Dostoevsky's *Crime and Punishment*—yet he also used the local library to tutor himself in the techniques of bookkeeping, and it was this self-

tuition that eventually brought him the job in Millwards Merchandising.

Hindley was a local girl, born in Manchester on July 23, 1942. Although unlike Brady her natural parents were together, she was brought up in a very tough household under a physically intimidating father, and soon came to accept violence as part of normal life. Nevertheless, she became a generally popular girl in the neighborhood, regularly baby-sitting for local families. Once she left school, she found employment in various administrative and clerical roles, which eventually took her to Millwards Merchandising.

Hindley's attempts to kindle a relationship with Brady initially met with disinterest, but eventually he warmed to her approaches. Their courting had something of a peculiar quality about it. Brady was quite open about his fascination with Nazi doctrine, and they spent time together reading books about Nazi atrocities or watching movies about German military history.

Much later in life, when applying to the British Home Secretary for parole in the 1970s, Hindley stated: "Within months he [Brady] had convinced me that there was no God at all: he could have told me that the earth was flat, the moon was made of green cheese and the sun rose in the west,

I would have believed him, such was his power of persuasion." Whatever the motivation behind these statements, there is no denying that Brady had a profound effect in reshaping this young woman's character. She began wearing more provocative clothing, dyed her hair white blonde to match the classic Aryan model, and at one point joined a local gun club so the couple could acquire firearms. Their sex life was also outlandish for the times, and included taking explicit photographs of each other, while also enjoying the works of the Marquis de Sade as intellectual fantasies. Yet so far this behavior was contained within their own relationship. Soon it would go well beyond these bounds.

▼ Although Myra Hindley caught the lion's share of press attention, Ian Brady was undoubtedly the motive force behind the series of murders, having a sadistic and ruthless character.

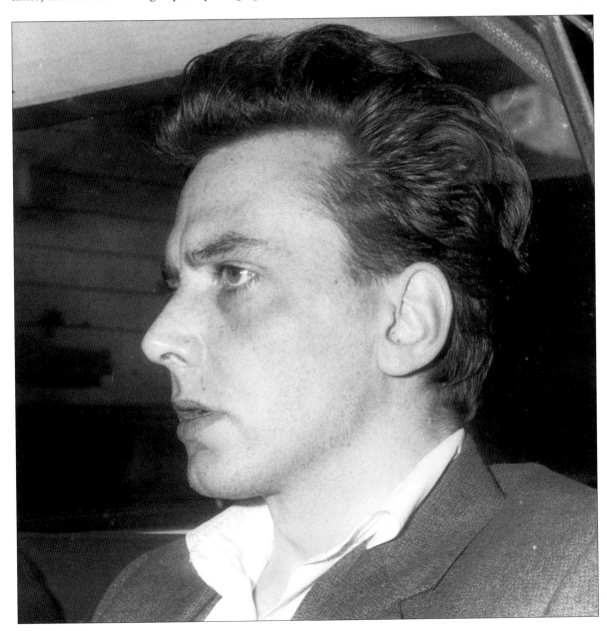

▼ A photograph of Myra Hindley, dressed in the clothing in which she assisted some of the murders. Brady would often use her as a lure for his victims, relying on the fact that murderous women were almost unthinkable in the 1960s.

PREYING ON THE YOUNG

It is hard to unravel the psychological complexities of how Myra Hindley and Ian Brady went from an undeniably dark and sensual relationship to a regular desire to commit murder. During another

appeal Hindley made for her release in 1997, Brady also wrote to the Home Secretary Jack Straw arguing against the idea that she was simply an innocent lamb drawn into evil. He stated in his letter:

"First accept the determinant. Myra Hindley and I once loved each other. We were a unified force, not two conflicting entities. The relationship was not based on the delusional concept of folie a deux, *but on a conscious/subconscious emotional and psychological affinity. She regarded periodic homicides as rituals of reciprocal innervation, marriage ceremonies theoretically binding us ever closer. As the records show, before we met my criminal activities had been primarily mercenary. Afterwards, a duality of motivation developed. Existential philosophy melded with the spirituality of death and became predominant. We experimented with the concept of total possibility. Instead of the requisite Lady Macbeth, I got Messalina. Apart our futures would have taken radically divergent courses."*

Putting aside the implications of Brady's evident intellectual fascination with his own condition, it is clear from the statement that he saw the murders they committed as part of a mutual and consensual experience, in which Hindley was a full and willing partner. It certainly seems from later behavior that Hindley and Brady crossed the line together.

The first murder occurred on July 12, 1963. The victim was 16-year-old Pauline Reade; Hindley managed to lure her up onto the remote Saddleworth Moor in the south Pennines, where Brady appears to have sexually assaulted her and then slit her throat. (See "Timeline of a Murder.") This first killing simply seemed to whet the couple's appetite for further murders. In addition, they now targeted their attentions on far younger victims. On November 23, they coaxed 12-year-old John Kilbride to go with them, using the promise of some extra pocket money if he helped them pack up some local market stands. His fate was also to end up sexually assaulted, murdered, and buried on Saddleworth Moor, and on June 16, 1964, 12-year-old Keith Bennett joined him, abducted as he was walking the short journey between his own home and his grandmother's house. Despite intensive police efforts to find these missing children, the victims seem to have disappeared into thin air.

The following December, the couple struck again, and this time Hindley's own involvement became even more integral to the murder. Ten-year-old Lesley Ann Downey was abducted from a fair, the helpful little girl having carried some of Hindley's shopping, which Hindley had pretended to drop. Instead of taking her straight up on to the moors, they took her home (Hindley and Brady had been living together since 1963), where they tied her up and took photographs of her being sexually assaulted. For their own twisted purposes, they even made an audio recording of the terrified girl's cries and pleas. She was then strangled, although it is unclear by whom. After her killing she was also buried on Saddleworth Moor.

WITNESS

Hindley and Brady would claim one more victim, but on this occasion it would lead to their arrest. For some reason, Brady began to believe that many other people would share his appetite for murder, including 17-year-old David Smith, the brother of Hindley's younger sister Maureen. Smith was undeniably impressed by the older Brady, taken in by his intelligent yet defiant persona. On October 6, 1965, Hindley asked David to walk her home to 16 Wardle Brook Avenue after a visit to his house. When they arrived, she invited David into the house, promising that she had some bottles of wine for him. While he stood in the kitchen, however, he heard a piercing scream. Rushing into the living room, he witnessed Brady swinging an axe and smashing it twice into the head of 17-year-old Edward Evans, whom Brady had met at Manchester station and invited to stay at his home. Brady ensured Evans was dead by throttling him with an electric appliance cord.

Brady and Hindley seemed to expect that Smith would approve of what he had just witnessed. They made him a cup of tea and sat around talking, Brady boasting about others he had killed and buried on Saddleworth Moor. (He had spoken to Smith previously about these murders, but at the time Smith believed that they were just fantasies.) Smith later went home, but in mental turmoil he told his wife and then, the next morning, they went to the police.

At first, the police found Smith's story outlandish, but respecting the possibility it might be true some two dozen officers went round to 16 Wardle Brook Avenue. Finding Hindley at home, they quickly gained access and in an upstairs bedroom discovered the battered body of Edward Evans, wrapped up in sheets, with the murder weapon nearby. Brady and Hindley were quickly arrested. During their initial interrogation, the couple attempted to pin much of the blame for the murder on David Smith, who had several prior convictions for assault, but based on what Smith had told them the police also conducted a thorough search of Saddleworth Moor.

Now the investigation had a critical break. During the search of the house at Wardle Brook Avenue, the police discovered a left-luggage ticket for a locker at Manchester Central Station. There they found two suitcases full of damning evidence, including explicit photographs of Lesley Ann Downey tied to the bed in Hindley's bedroom, the 13-minute tape recording of Downey's violent end, plus a photograph of Hindley squatting down over what would prove to be the grave of John Kilbride. Using the evidence of the photographs, the police were able to discover the bodies of both Kilbride and Downey. The police were now fully aware that the couple were probably responsible for the

Timeline of Two Murderers—Known Victims of Ian Brady and Myra Hindley

DATE	VICTIM	AGE	DETAILS
July 12, 1963	Pauline Reade	16	Lured onto Saddleworth Moor by Myra Hindley, where she was sexually assaulted and where either Brady alone murdered her, or did so with Hindley's assistance.
November 23, 1963	John Kilbride	12	Abducted from a market at Ashton-under-Lyne, and forced into the back of a hired Ford Anglia. He was taken to Saddleworth Moor, sexually assaulted, then had his throat slit and was strangled.
June 16, 1964	Keith Bennett	12	Disappeared while walking to his grandmother's house in Gorton; was lured into a car by Hindley, taken to Saddleworth Moor, and murdered. His body has never been found.
December 26, 1964	Lesley Ann Downey	10	Abducted from a fairground and taken to Brady's house; there she was sexually assaulted and murdered; Hindley and Brady took explicit photographs of Downey and made an audio recording during her murder.
October 6, 1965	Edward Evans	17	Killed with an axe at Brady's house, in the presence of a third party, David Smith; Smith subsequently reported the incident to the police, starting the criminal investigation that led to the arrest and conviction of Hindley and Brady.

disappearance of other children, but they were only able to charge them with the murders of Downey, Kilbride, and Evans.

TRIAL AND JUDGEMENT

Myra Hindley and Ian Brady were brought to trial on April 27, 1966 at Chester Assizes, where they continued to protest their innocence and point the finger at Smith. The evidence gathered against them, particularly the tape recording (which clearly contained their voices), was damning, however. The outcome was that Brady was found guilty of all three murders and Hindley was found guilty of two murders, that of Lesley Ann Downey and Edward Evans. They were both sentenced to life imprisonment; had they been convicted of their crimes just a few months previously they would have received the death sentence (capital punishment was abolished in Great Britain in 1965).

During the early years of their imprisonment, Brady and Hindley continued as a loving couple, writing to each other and requesting permission to marry. Time divided them, however, with Hindley continuing to protest her innocence and blaming Brady, while Brady himself accepted his guilt but attacked the view that Hindley was a victim rather than a perpetrator. Hindley began a long and highly publicized series of appeals, even taking her case as far as the European Court of Human Rights. No level of the judiciary found her explanations plausible, and Brady did his best to highlight her involvement in every aspect of the murders, including claiming that it was she who strangled Lesley Ann Downey (the most plausible version of events when compared against the evidence of the tape recording). Having had her original 30-year sentence extended to full life in the 1990s, Myra

▲ April 1966. Senior detectives arrive at court for the trial of Ian Brady and Myra Hindley. The police were able to produce photographic and audio recordings to corroborate the prosecution's case, and the murderers were left with little on which to pin their defense.

Hindley died in prison of bronchial pneumonia and heart disease on November 15, 2002.

Ian Brady continues to serve out his sentence in Ashworth Psychiatric Hospital, Liverpool. Of his victims, the body of Pauline Reade was discovered in 1987, after Hindley and Brady themselves went back to the moor to help police in a fresh search. The body of Keith Bennett has never been found, a lasting torment for the family.

THE HILLSIDE STRANGLERS

The lives of Kenneth (Kenny) Bianchi and Angelo Buono—better known to history as the "Hillside Stranglers"—are both stories of a deep-seated pathological hatred of women. That two individuals would share the same outlook, and the desire to express it in murder, makes these men a distinctive case in the history of serial killers.

On October 17, 1977, a 19-year-old prostitute called Yolanda Washington climbed into a car in Los Angeles. Inside the car were cousins, Kenny Bianchi and Angelo Buono, and they weren't happy. They were trying out a new career as pimps, and a month previously they thought they had made their first smart move when a woman called Deborah Noble sold them a list of men known to use prostitutes.

◀ Kenneth Bianchi, one of the Hillside Stranglers, here testifies in court against his cousin and accomplice Angelo Buono. Once they were arrested, any loyalty between the pair quickly dissolved.

Timeline of a Murder

1: Thursday January 11, 1979, 7 P.M. Twenty-two-year-old student *Karen Mandic* finishes work for the day at the Fred Myer department store on Interstate 5, Bellingham, Washington. She works there as a part-time cashier.

2: Earlier in the week, Kenneth Bianchi offered Karen $100 to house-sit in a Bayside house that he was watching over as a security guard, the ostensible purpose being that she should wait in until the arrival of some burglar alarm repair people in the evening. Karen told two friends about the arrangement; they were both concerned, but she reassured them that everything was fine and that she would take a friend, *Diane Wilder*, with her.

3: Shortly after 7 P.M., Karen and Diane arrive at the location given by Bianchi. He begins to show them separately around the house, then forces them one at a time down some stairs into the basement.

4: Bianchi's later confession, to the author Christopher Berry-Dee, ran as follows: "They were told to lay face down and then they were separated, tied up and, individually, one by one, untied, undressed, and I had sex with them. Then they were both dressed again. Then I killed them separately [by strangulation]. I believe, ah, Diane Wilder was first and Karen Mandic second. Then they were carried out and put in the back of the car and driven to the cul-de-sac."
(From Christopher Berry-Dee, *Face to Face with Serial Killers,* John Blake, 2007)

5: The two girls are quickly reported missing, and their bodies are discovered in the trunk of a car in a cul-de-sac in Willow Drive. Although Bianchi initially denied knowing the two girls, a note in Karen's campus room listed his name and phone number—when police rang the number, Bianchi answered. Combined with other evidence, they were able to make an arrest.

All they had to do was match girls with the names, go on the sell, and the money would start rolling in.

When Deborah passed over the list to the two men, she was accompanied by her friend Yolanda Washington, the meeting planting her face in Bianchi and Buono's memory. The girls then left, having received payment for the list, which the men quickly discovered consisted of nothing but false names. They had been duped. Yolanda may have been simply a friend, and not party to the deceit, but when Bianchi and Buono couldn't find Deborah Noble, she took the brunt of their anger. In the back of the car, away from prying eyes, she was violently raped and assaulted and then strangled to death with a ligature. Her body was casually discarded, dumped in a cemetery.

Yolanda Washington was the first victim of the Hillside Stranglers, the first of 12 unfortunate women to meet such a fate. Arguably, Yolanda was killed for revenge. From then on, however, Bianchi and Buono would kill for pleasure.

MUTUAL INTERESTS

Kenneth Bianchi was born many miles away from Los Angeles, in New York on May 22, 1951. His natural birth mother was a prostitute who gave away the unwanted child immediately, and he was adopted by Nicholas Bianchi and his wife Frances, who was Kenny's aunt by birth, when he was three months old. In his early years, Kenny had a variety of puzzling medical complaints that stretched the patience of his adoptive parents. He scarcely slept, and suffered from chronic incontinence. He also seemed to lapse into strange trances during which his eyes would roll back in his head. His mental state varied between inattentiveness and anger, and although he had a decent IQ (116) when it was measured at 11 years old, he did poorly in school.

Between his early teens and early 20s, Kenny went through several key formative experiences. His father died suddenly, when Kenny was 13. At the age of 18, he married one Brenda Beck, having had an earlier marriage proposal rejected by another girl. The marriage was disastrous, and broke up after eight months when she left him without explanation. Filled with resentment toward women and life, Bianchi then went through a series of dead-end jobs, making some extra money by stealing from apartments and stores while working as a

▶ The trial of Bianchi and Buono was a highly charged affair. Here Kenneth Bianchi bursts into tears as he admits to a series of murders, although he would blame his actions on a split personality.

security guard. Finally, he had had enough of life in New York and decided to move to Los Angeles, where he had a contact in the form of his adoptive cousin, Angelo Buono.

The two men hit it off immediately, despite being a visually curious pairing. Bianchi was

▼ A police officer escorts Angelo Buono (right) into Buono's upholstery store in Glendale, California, to conduct a search warrant. The LAPD established a dedicated Hillside Strangler Task Force.

undeniably attractive, with dark and engaging features. Buono, by contrast, was not what you'd call a classically handsome man, although a certain charisma and style made him a big hit with women. Buono was born on October 5, 1934, and moved to California at the age of five after his parents divorced. For reasons unclear, by his early teens Buono had developed a violent sexuality, fantasizing about attacking women and idolizing local rapists who appeared in the news. No surprise, therefore, that he had trouble holding down normal relationships. Between 1955 and 1972 he was married and divorced/or separated four times, and had numerous children, some of whom he sexually abused, including rapes perpetrated on one of his daughters. On several occasions he also threatened to kill his wives, especially as they began divorce proceedings. He was a truly disturbed individual—on one occasion in the 1970s his roommate saw him standing at the window masturbating as he watched schoolchildren outside through binoculars. The pairing with Bianchi in 1975 was bound to lead to no good.

FROM BUSINESS TO PLEASURE

Based on a mutual twisted interest in women plus a desire for illegal gains, the two men quickly decided to attempt pimping as a shared career. They initially attempted to work a couple of girls, Sabra Hannan and Becky Spears, but both women quickly realized the nature of their managers, who kept them as virtual prisoners, and managed to get away. The ill-fated Deborah Noble alliance was the next move, which led directly to their first murder.

The killing of Yolanda Washington seems to have been a trigger for the two men to explore their deepest and most sadistic desires. On October 31, 1977, they decided to relive the experience. This time the victim was 15-year-old prostitute Judith Miller. Her violated body was discovered in the pleasant middle-class residential area of La Crescenta, the girl having been bound at the wrists and ankles and then cruelly strangled. It was

unlikely that the killing actually took place in La Crescenta, so it appeared that whoever murdered her dumped her in an area that would deliberately taunt both respectable society and the police. Furthermore, the ligature marks around the wrists, ankles, and throat would soon become the identifying characteristic of the Hillside Stranglers' murders.

Bodies now began to stack up thick and fast. On November 5, Bianchi and Buono killed their third victim, Elissa Kastin, a 21-year-old waitress who was just teetering on the brink of a move into prostitution. She had been raped, sodomized, and

Timeline of Two Murderers—Known Victims of Bianchi and Buono

DATE	VICTIM	AGE	DETAILS
October 17, 1977	Yolanda Washington	19	Bianchi and Buono's first murder victim; found with the strangulation ligature still around her neck.
October 31, 1977	Judith Ann Miller	15	Body found wrapped in a tarpaulin and dumped in downtown Los Angeles.
November 6, 1977	Elissa Kastin	21	Body bore ligature marks almost identical to those found on the previous two victims.
November 10, 1977	Jane King	28	Decomposed body not found until November 23, near an off ramp on the Golden State freeway.
November 13, 1977	Dolores Cepeda	12	Both girls were last seen talking to two men seated
	Sonja Johnson	14	in a car, after the girls had stepped off the schoolbus on their way home; both girls were raped and strangled.
November 20, 1977	Kristin Weckler	20	Body indicated signs of torture, including puncture holes from attempts at lethal injection.
November 29, 1977	Lauren Wagner	18	Burn marks on her hands indicated signs of electrical torture.
December 9, 1977	Kimberley Martin	18	Raped and strangled.
February 17, 1978	Cindy Lee Hudspeth	20	Body found in the trunk of a car that had been pushed over a cliff.

Murders committed by Bianchi alone

| January 11, 1979 | Karen Mandic | 22 | both girls are raped and murdered after Bianchi lured them |
| | Diane Wilder | 27 | into a house he was watching over as a security guard. |

strangled. The primary detective investigating these murders, Sergeant Frank Salerno, began to believe that the bodies were the product of the same killers; based on the way the bodies were moved, he correctly judged that two men were involved. He soon had more evidence to work with. Between November 9, 1977, and February 17, 1978, Bianchi and Buono killed another seven women with

▼ Bianchi is moved under LAPD escort during his trial in 1979. Bianchi was an intelligent man, but also an angry individual who found it hard to restrain his rage and his baser appetites.

increasing brutality and inventiveness. The critical element of these new murders, however, was that the two men were now starting to target women in general, not just prostitutes.

Furthermore, they also dipped into the realms of child murder. Two of their murders were committed on November 13, and their victims were 14-year-old Sonja Johnson and 12-year-old Dolores Cepeda. Other victims included college students and aspiring actresses. It was later revealed that the two men lured their victims into a car by posing as police officers, including wearing fake ID badges. As time went on, furthermore, the killers began

experimenting with new methods of torture and murder, including carbon monoxide poisoning and electrocution, although strangulation seems the only method with which they had success.

By now all of Los Angeles was talking about the "Hillside Strangler," so called because of the hilly, wooded location in which most of the bodies had been found. A police task force was set up to investigate the murders, and the LA Sheriff's Department and the LAPD managed to work closely together, contrary to the usual difficulties with such cooperation. Yet a significant breakthrough eluded the investigation. Furthermore, after the last murder, that of Cindy Hudspeth on February 17, the killers suddenly seemed to stop their campaign of terror. Why Bianchi and Buono chose to rein themselves in at this moment is uncertain, but it was possibly a combination of the desire to evade justice, plus the fact that Bianchi's current girlfriend had just given birth to a baby. Bianchi moved out to Bellingham, Washington, with his new family, where he worked as a security guard in a hardware store. This physical separation meant that the Hudspeth murder was the last that the two men committed together.

It was not Bianchi's last murder, however. On January 11, 1979, Kenneth Bianchi's burning desire to kill resurfaced. On this occasion, Bianchi perpetrated a double murder, luring two young college students into a house that he was guarding, where they were subsequently tied up, raped, and strangled. This time, however, Bianchi had been extremely careless in covering his tracks. Police discovered the bodies of the two girls in an abandoned car in woodland, and obtained valuable forensic evidence. Most critically, the police soon gained evidence that implicated Bianchi in the girls' disappearance (see "Timeline of a Murder" box). Bianchi was quickly in police custody, and a search of his house revealed jewelry belonging to two of the women killed in Los Angeles, Yolanda Washington and Kimberley Martin. In apprehending Bianchi for the Bellingham murders, the police had also opened the door on the case of the Hillside Stranglers.

EVASION AND CONVICTION
Charged with murder, Kenneth Bianchi now began a bizarre psychological game, seeking to avoid culpability. He attempted to convince police and psychiatrists that he actually had multiple personality disorder, and the murders were really committed by one of his alter egos, "Steve Walker." This construction was actually nothing more than an elaborate ruse, although for a time several forensic psychiatrists were taken in. Eventually, however, his over-complicated attempt at psychological deceit came unstuck when he suddenly introduced a third personality based on what psychiatrist had told him about multiple personality disorders. Having been discovered, Bianchi gave up Buono without hesitation, and on October 22, 1979 Buono was arrested.

While both men were incarcerated and awaiting trial, a bizarre incident occurred. A clearly unstable female fan of the Hillside Stranglers, 23-year-old Veronica Lynn Compton, began corresponding with Bianchi, under the pretense that she was researching information for a play about a female serial killer. Secretly, the pair hatched a plot in which Compton would actually murder a victim on Bianchi's behalf, planting his semen at the scene—Bianchi passed her some of his semen in a rubber glove when she visited him in prison on September 16, 1980. The plot came badly unstuck when Compton actually attempted the murder; she was overpowered by her victim, and her attempts to actually cover her tracks and free Bianchi led to nothing but her eventual arrest and imprisonment.

MARATHON TRIAL
During the trial of Bianchi and Buono between 1981 and 1983, Bianchi in particular tried to wriggle free of responsibility by once again attempting to play mind games with the court. Yet ultimately both a judge and jury saw through his attempts, and in November 1983, after one of the longest trials in U.S. history, both men were convicted of multiple murders and received life imprisonment.

Kenneth Bianchi is still serving his sentence in Washington State Penitentiary, while Angelo Buono died of a heart attack in Calipatria State Prison on September 21, 2002. As the court case had revealed, although the two men had been accomplices in murder, the only thing that united them was a sick desire to kill, and there was no mutual loyalty.

FRED AND ROSEMARY WEST

Most serial killers work alone, although on occasions close family members may suspect their activities. In the deeply disturbing case of Rosemary and Fred West, however, we encounter two people of equal depravity, whose own house and backyard became the main venue for the torture, rape, murder, and burial of at least 12 girls and young women.

T he story of what happened at 25 Cromwell Street, Gloucester, U.K., begins in the childhoods of two people, Fred and Rosemary West. Fred West was born on September 29, 1941 in Bickerton Cottage, Much Marcle, Herefordshire, the second son of Walter Stephen West and his wife Daisy. Later in life, Fred would claim that his childhood exposed him to incest, pedophilia, and bestiality through his father,

◀ A police forensics team digs up the garden at 25 Cromwell St., Gloucester, in 1994. In total, nine badly decayed, mutilated bodies were found in the backyard alone, with more remains in the house's cellar.

▲ Ten of the girls murdered by the Wests over a 24-year period: 1. Therese Siegenthaler 2. Charmaine West 3. Heather West 4. Shirley Anne Robinson 5. Shirley Hubbard 6. Lynda Gough 7. Juanita Mott 8. Lucy Partington 9. Carol Ann Cooper 10. Alison Chambers.

although Fred's habitual lying often makes it hard to unpack what actually occurred in his early years. Certainly, something seems to have gone wrong in the young man from an early age. He had extremely poor literacy, a problem that would dog him for the rest of his life. Following a serious motorbike accident in November 1958, which put him in a lengthy coma, Fred's personality seems to have warped, and he began to show tendencies of sexual predation and violent rage. He got into trouble with the police for minor acts of theft, and at the age of 20 he was charged with having sex with a minor (a 13-year-old girl). The defense claim that Fred suffered from epileptic fits managed to save him from jail time, but his troubled relationship with females had now emphatically begun.

Although Fred was by no means normal, he managed to develop an attractive and apparently trustworthy character, and was popular with women. In 1962, Fred struck up a relationship with a young woman, Catherine Costello, better known as Rena, and they moved to Scotland after a secret marriage. Catherine was already pregnant by a previous relationship when she began going out with Fred, and once in Scotland she gave birth to a daughter, Charmaine, in March 1963. The arrival of a child did not reform Fred in the slightest. As well as making Rena's life a misery through constant demands for unconventional sex, Fred also had a series of casual relationships with the teenage girls who flocked around the ice cream van that he drove as a job. The turbulent marriage produced Fred's own child, Anna Marie, but she was not enough to keep the pair together. Fred took up with Anna McFall, Rena's friend, and she too became pregnant. Now Fred's life was about to take a different course.

NEW HORIZONS

In early 1967, probably in response to her insistence that he actually divorce Rena (Fred was a tremendously possessive man), Fred murdered Anna McFall, dismembered her pregnant body and buried her not far from the trailer in which they were living. (Fred had learned how to butcher meat while working in a slaughterhouse.) He also cut off and removed her fingers and toes, an act that would become a trademark of his later murders. Rena moved back in with the precarious Fred, but noted that he was beginning to abuse Charmaine, touching her inappropriately. Evidence also suggests that around this time he was responsible for several sexual assaults on young women in the area, including the abduction of 15-year-old Mary Bastholm from a bus stop in Gloucester and her subsequent murder. He was certainly in constant scrapes with the police and women, but he would

soon have a new relationship in his life.

In late November 1968, Fred met Rosemary Pauline Letts. Born in Barnstaple, Devon, on November 29, 1953, Rosemary was another troubled individual. A misfit in school, she was sexually abused by her father. Rose was also a sexually adventurous young woman, and there was an instant chemistry between her and Fred, despite his being 12 years her senior.

Much to her father's anger, Rose moved in with Fred at the age of 16, and was left caring for Charmaine and Anna Marie while Fred spent periods in jail for various crimes. They also had a child together—Heather was born in 1970.

As the future would show, Fred was a monster, but he had found his equal in Rose. She was violently aggressive toward Charmaine in particular, and in the summer of 1971, during a ferocious argument, she beat and throttled the child to death. Fred was in jail at the time of the murder, but on his release shortly

Timeline of a Murder—June 1987

1: Fred West has a violent argument with his 16-year-old daughter, *Heather*, at their home at 25 Cromwell Street, Gloucester.

2: The argument intensifies, and Heather laughs in Fred's face. He slaps her across the face, then grabs her around the throat and begins to strangle her. Eventually she turns blue and stops breathing.

3: According to Fred, he now attempted to revive Heather by running cold water over her in the bathtub. The attempt did not work, and so Fred dragged her from the bathtub, stripped off her clothes and looked to dispose of the body.

4: He initially attempts to dispose of the body completely, stuffing it in a large garbage can outside. The body does not fit, so he takes it back into the house to cut up.

5: Before he begins the dismemberment of his own daughter, Fred strangles her again with a pair of tights to make sure she is dead. He then saws off her head and limbs with a large knife, and stuffs the body parts back into the garbage can.

6: In the middle of the night, Fred goes out into the backyard and buries Heather's body. It would not be discovered for seven years.

afterward he helped Rose bury the child beneath their house on Midland Road. Her body would remain there for 20 years.

Soon Fred himself would have another opportunity to kill. Eventually his former wife Rena grew suspicious at Charmaine's absence. She turned up at the house in Midland Road in August 1971. She soon joined her daughter in death. Fred murdered her, cut off her fingers and toes (as he had done to Charmaine), and buried her in bags close to the location of Anna McFall's body.

MARRIED MURDERERS

By the time that Fred and Rosemary West were married in January 1972, both of them were murderers. Yet this was just the beginning. Life inside the home became utterly perverted from normality. Sexual relations between the couple involved violence and degradation, and Fred would hire out Rose as a prostitute, even to his own father, and watch her activities through holes in the walls. At one point they drugged and raped their young neighbor, Elizabeth Agius.

Six months after they married, they had another child, called Mae West. They also moved shortly afterward to 25 Cromwell Road, to which Fred was particularly attracted on account of its large cellar, which he planned to turn into a soundproofed torture chamber. The house was also big enough to accommodate lodgers, and with their large family the Wests would soon have a string of unfortunate young women staying with them as nannies. From

now on, violence and killing would become an integral feature of their sex life.

It began with their own children. Anna Marie was violently raped by Fred on several occasions, often while Rose held her down. Then they abducted and sexually assaulted 17-year-old nanny Caroline Owens, who nonetheless managed to avoid death and escaped to tell the police. Tragically, although the Wests were taken to court, the judge believed their protestations that Caroline was a willing participant in their sex games, despite Fred's record, and the pair remained free to commit further outrages.

The first killing at 25 Cromwell Street was that of 19-year-old Lynda Gough, also hired as a nanny. In April 1973, she was tortured and murdered before being dismembered and buried beneath the garage. She was far from the last. From December 1973 to June 1987, eight other women were murdered in what became a ghastly killing house. Whether abducted from the street, or lured into the house on false pretenses, they suffered terrible fates at the hands of a merciless couple. In one instance (Shirley Hubbard, murdered November 1974), the victim had her head wrapped entirely in duct tape, with just a short rubber tube projecting from her

▶ Fred and Rose West pose for the camera. Fred began dating Rose when she was only 15, and she moved in with him at the age of 16. They were both violent individuals in their own right, and fused their capacity for murder with a twisted sex life.

mouth to allow her to breathe. Another victim was tied up with excruciating ligatures and suspended from the cellar ceiling. One woman (Shirley Anne Robinson, murdered May 1978) was actually killed after becoming pregnant with Fred's child.

After the murder of Alison Chambers in August 1979, a curious thing happened. The murders seem to stop, for reasons that are still unclear. As far as

▼ Rose West is transported to court for her trial in 1994. She resisted any sort of confession, preferring to present herself as a victim of Fred's manipulation, but circumstantial evidence against her was conclusive.

we know, no more people were killed for another eight years, but in June 1987 the Wests committed one final atrocity. Their last victim was their own daughter, Heather, who was murdered and whose body was buried under the patio in the garden. Fred used to threaten his remaining children (Rose had three more, not all with Fred) with the same fate should they ever tell anybody about what went on in Cromwell Road.

DISCOVERY

Yet in the end that is exactly what happened. In August 1992, police received allegations that Fred

Timeline of Two Murderers—Known Victims of Fred and Rosemary West

DATE	VICTIM	AGE	DETAILS
February 22, 1963	Charmaine West	8	Murdered by Rosemary West. Fred helps Rose dispose of the body.
August 1971	Catherine West	17	Catherine Bernadette "Rena" West is murdered by Fred after she enquired about her daughter Charmaine's whereabouts.
April 1973	Lynda Gough	19	Killed while living as a lodger at 25 Cromwell Street.
November 1973	Carol Ann Cooper	15	Murdered by the Wests after being abducted while walking home from the movies.
December 1973	Lucy Katherine Partington	21	Killed by the Wests after abducting her from a bus station. She was been kept alive for least several days before her murder.
April 1974	Theresa Siegenthaler	21	Murdered after disappearing on a hitchhiking trip to Ireland.
November 1974	Shirley Hubbard	16	Abducted and murdered after finishing her work experience course in Droitwich.
April 1975	Juanita Marion Mott	17	A former lodger at 25 Cromwell Street, who later disappeared while living with her friend in Newent.
May 1978	Shirley Anne Robinson	18	Worked as a prostitute for the Wests, and was murdered after becoming pregnant with Fred's child.
August 1979	Alison Chambers	16	The last of the West murders for nearly eight years.
June 1987	Heather Ann West	16	Killed because, in Fred's words, she had been "sneering" at him.

was engaged in child abuse, and police searches of their house found videos of Fred and Rose engaged in violent sexual assaults on children. Furthermore, the younger children, who had been taken into care by social services, let slip that their sister Heather was buried under the patio. When police explored this lead, the subsequent search opened up a house of horrors. A total of nine bodies were found in the garden, and others in the cellar.

Fred West made several confusing confessions and retractions, but the evidence was overwhelming, and on June 30, 1994 he was charged with 11 counts of murder and Rose was charged with 10 counts. Fred would ultimately escape justice. Although he had confessed to most

of the murders, Rose quickly realized that he would drag her down with him, so attempted to present herself as a powerless victim of his monstrous personality. Abandoned by his partner in crime, Fred West hanged himself on January 1, 1995, using the bedsheets in his prison cell in Birmingham as a noose. Rose, nevertheless, was put on trial. Although the case was now circumstantial, a strong body of witnesses plus video evidence led to a sure conviction, and on November 22, 1995, the jury found her guilty on all counts by a unanimous verdict. As if bringing the whole horrifying episode to a close, the trial judge, Mr. Justice Mantell, when sentencing her to life imprisonment noted "If attention is paid to what I think, you will never be released."

INDEX

Page numbers in *italics* refer to illustrations.
Numbers in **bold** refer to information in boxes.
Not all the victims are listed in the index, only those with additional information about them.